Collected Poems

Marya Zaturenska

The Viking Press, New York

First published in 1965 by The Viking Press, Inc.,
625 Madison Avenue, New York, N.Y. 10022.

Published simultaneously in Canada by
The Macmillan Company of Canada Limited.

Library of Congress catalog card number: 65-23955

Set in Bodoni Book, Electra, and Bank Script
and printed in U.S.A. by The Vail-Ballou Press, Inc.
Design: M. B. Glick

The poem "Cascades and Fountains," on page 3, is from *Terraces of Light*. Poems from that volume and from *Selected Poems* are used by permission of the publisher, Grove Press, Inc.

Collected Poems

Marya Zaturenska

Also by Marya Zaturenska

POETRY

Threshold and Hearth
Cold Morning Sky
The Listening Landscape
The Golden Mirror
Selected Poems
Terraces of Light

PROSE

Christina Rossetti: A Portrait with Background
A History of American Poetry, 1900–1940
  (*with Horace Gregory*)

ANTHOLOGIES (with Horace Gregory)

The Crystal Cabinet: An Introduction to Poetry
The Mentor Book of Religious Verse
The Silver Swan: Poems of Mystery and Imagination

TO THE MEMORY OF *Pascal Covici*

Contents

viii

FROM Selected Poems

FROM Terraces of Light

New Poems

Collected Poems

Marya Zaturenska

Cascades and Fountains

Drawn from deep sleep, the dark, dim waters run,
Fountains of living waters night and day
That wash my life away.
Surely they gush from the dry rock, the thirsty sun,
Splendid and fertile, spraying the dead grass
With light as in a golden fastness.

Slow life, and slower change, muted, immutable,
Running like water quick and shallow, clear:
Dark year on hurrying year—
Beneath the glowing heaven, under the nimble heels
Of rushing worlds you keep
All that the sleepy and resentful dreamscape feels.

Fons rejuventutis,
                healing flood—
The pure limbs of beauty enter you,
Energy fresh and brilliant, the reviving blood,
Warm eyes and springing hair
Meet in your flood, dissolve and are united there,
While the wild waters flood time's crumbling stair.

Toward the Atlantis of the soul you move:
Worlds flung underseas, an abyss closed and sealed,
Sources of life forgotten and revealed,
Foam alleluias rising from above
In watery peals of love,
Unlocking passions like a choral flood
That sings within the blood.

FROM *Threshold and Hearth*

1934

"City Trees in April," on page 18, has not previously been published but was written during the same period as the poems from *Threshold and Hearth*.

All Soul's Eve

This house held all the summer in:
On the appointed eve she came
Wrapped in a winding sheet of flame;
My breath was but a sudden pang
Remembered through awakening
And through the doors there seemed to cling
A pale, dark aura wild and thin,
And a metallic clang.

Then she came down the wooden stairs,
On the black railing was her hand;
From out the outer world she came,
The world of silence and despair
Dissolved around her like a flame
And all the silence cried, "Beware."

Till in my blood the thought of death
Shook in dark meaning like a storm
That drives the doomed ship live and warm
Out of the known, beloved breath.
I saw descending the black stairs
The ghost through whom my spirit lives,
The unborn child, heir of my heirs
And all by which the future thrives.

Then close small house, dimmed windows close,
And my two eyes, till morning break
Seek only silence and repose,
Remembering heaven for her sake.
By charms that the death-angel knows
Beseech her to return alone
To her forgotten dwelling-place.
Lest we remembering her face

Yearn only for that heavenly rose
And that eternal tropic sky:
Learn to forget that we must die
And scorn the season of the snows.

After Saint Teresa

Let nothing disturb you,
Nothing affright you,
The Great Shadow
Will swallow the world,
The desert thirsty
With endless longing,
The mountains breathing
Remotest air,
The earth who mothers
All living creatures,
All move in Time
To an unknown end.

Let Silence clothe you,
Let Silence seal
Your lips with wisdom,
Your heart with zeal;
Your body move
In an ancient quiet
Wordless, yet weighted
With thought, with love.

Chorale for Autumn

The leaves of autumn burning through the gray
Are you, dark head, stilled blood and perilous tongue.
Burn, O thin trees and in small gardens scatter
Your leaves that on reluctant branches stay.

How many seasons has this tamed heart known
Lashing the hounds of fall to the bare hills,
Hallowing among the shadows of a dream—
The bright leaves lying where the flowers have been!

Gather the chilled days in, let the calm house,
Of peace, entreat, enclose, and comfort them.
The days burn cold and high, the sheaves are in,
Prepare, O Death, to hold your last carouse.

The world grows cool as amber and as clear;
That which is dark grows light; the sunlight stands,
Obscure as anguish worn out by sharp time,
As a leaf in its season falls the year.

Another Autumn

Another autumn shines on the grave hills
And the hot earth breathes quietly again.
Like an old book, much read and greatly loved,
The thoughtful day lifts high its luminous head.

The thoughtful day its luminous head lifts high,
As burning colors slowly drain the trees
And burning thoughts return
To nourish slowly-chilling ecstasies.

The slowly-chilling ecstasies remain
Locked in the heart's casket secretly,
Though the sharp air can move the eager blood
Grown tense to meet the brightly-changing year.

Grown tense to meet the year so brightly changed,
Grown clairvoyant with the spell that makes
Metallic mystery on turgid lakes
And ruddy splendor on the dying leaves.

Fulfillment

I have reached Willowsleigh through what strange passes.
Through endless desolations I remembered
Your sky-swept walks, your bright unearthly flowers.
The City of God, the village known in dreams
Is mine; I walk the unforgotten grasses.

The seasons pass, the sun stands high and still
As through a crystal my tall neighbors go
Walled in by desolate quiet, bound yet free:
The grass is up, then gone, and Spring comes and Decem-
    ber,
The heat, the frost, the fragrance, the rain and the snow.

Daphne

Roots spring from my feet, Apollo, like a tree
The silver laurels grow deep into me;
Undone, undone, these thoughts of mine that beat
With a great vigor in the drouth and heat;
So my blood answers, so with sap my veins,
So as leaves in whom no wind complains,
This is the metamorphosis, this the change
Through which my days now range:
That which was I, am now no longer I,
Among my branches let the wild birds cry,
Around me let the alien rivers flow,
Beneath my shade let other maidens go.

The Scythe, The Spindle, and the Cypress Tree

By that bright stream that flows,
Where no man knows,
You knelt in anguish of the sultry day
To drink in cooling draughts your life away.

Over your lost and beautiful young head
I saw the ancient symbols of the dead,
The scythe, the spindle, and the cypress tree,
And they were drowsy with eternity.

"Arise," I cried. "And look awhile on me."
The years will rain upon the cypress tree,
The years will drop like lead into this pool,
Upon your golden thoughts the years will rust,
Upon your golden life will fall the dust.

You looked at me with eyes that pierced through
    clouds,
I saw the generations in their shrouds.
You smiled on me as though
You knew the path through which my feet will go.
And O the beautiful young cypress tree
That flowed through you, and was a part of me,
And O the magical leaves that sigh and sing,
"You are our Lord, our Warrior, and our King."
Come back, O beautiful and tender one.
Restore us to the long-forgotten sun.

The Uninvited Guest

Through what doors will you enter, through what
    walls
Will your white soul resume its solitudes?
I count the clockbeats in my mind, the warning
    trumpet
Reëchoing in my heart and hear no answer,
No answer and no cry
And no reply.

On a known hour at an appointed rendezvous
(So destiny has spoken)
Your eloquent feet will sing in the dry grass;
I know their rhythm cruel and sweet
And their presaging beat
On that unknown street.

Surprise will come like a stern robber,
Fear like a jealous pain, and joy
Come carrying gifts disastrous and rich—
Yet I shall miss
That steep abyss.

Where shall I wait, where shall impatience lie,
On what low bed of thorns will my head rest
Until I meet the uninvited guest,
Will the door open at a secret word
Unknown, unheard?

Shall I run down the world whose strict restraint
Held me too long, whose iron hand has left
Its sharp stigmata on my brows and heart?
See I have waited long, the golden lamp I light
Through the expectant night.

O Lyric March

FOR MELINDA

The cold and violent wind of March
Cuts sharply through this little world
Obscured by the long snow, and a small room
Where quiet melted into gloom.

And then you came yourself, tall lady,
Your hands with fresh flowers, your eyes like birds,
Bright forerunner of song, dispeller of cloud,
Delicate and proud.

Joy for the white arbutus trembling through
The melting, quivering earth and shyly stirring
The shivering tendrils of the grass
To deeper happiness.

Faint mellow sun, young sky too wistful now,
Freshen this little room, this little house,
Where iron winter kept too close a guard
In her severest mood,
A marble solitude.

That Field So Green

That field so green, so green,
In the sun's graying gold
Once seen, now never seen,
That world, that path so green!

A girl could run and hide
In its large shadows, know
The flesh stripped from her pride,
And passion cooled like snow.

Feel death stir in her side,
Like a gray bird, feel peace,
Make her his silent bride,
In that lost field so green.

City Trees in April

The trees are feathery green, they blow in air
Like fluttering ballet skirts, or green umbrellas,
Or a pale woman's long and trailing hair—
The young trees in city streets are Cinderellas.

Beautiful among the cinders and the dry soot of the streets
They lift light heads to heaven, young and cool,
Till one dreams beholding them of fields of wheat,
Or a fragrant walled-in garden, or a running country pool.

FROM *Cold Morning Sky*

1937

The Virgin, the Doe, and the Leper

They are always there:
The frightened virgin at the burning fountain,
The leper left upon the fatal stair,
The milk-white doe lost on the savage mountain.

Do you not hear them cry?
Despair and shame, that final sense
Of doom descending upon innocence,
Outcasts from pity's gentle eye?

I fly their shadowy pain;
I invoke the guardians of their destiny,
Angels of thunder and rain,
To keep sick pity from corrupting me.

Earth would deny them;
As I deny and plead, earth pleads, denies:
"O pitiful, stain not my garment's hem
And hide from me the silent wound that bleeds."

For are we not lost, too?
Are we not outcasts from time's living flood?
And often from the sky's deceptive blue
Rains down a shower of blood.

When shelter seemed most near, and love most close,
When summer's golden eyelids opened wide,

Have we not seen the worm crawl from the rose?
Have we not seen the shadowy sisters glide?

Fatal and wan on cherished garden walks,
Whose was that sudden cry? that burning chill?
What halts our footsteps? and what stilled our talks?
What shadow stalks us, run wherever we will?

The Lunar Tides

Danger stalks on such nights, the moon is dangerous:
Why will you walk beneath the compelling luster
That draws the blood from your unwilling body?
The vampire moon with yellow streams of light
Drains the dim waters, sucks the moist air dry,
Casts cloudy spectres on the window pane—
The dead arise and walk again.

Oh, love, how are we drawn
Into this moon, this face as cold,
Remorseless as ambition, chilled with fever,
Burning with war that on these lunar tides
Draws all life to its danger; beautiful
It mocks the living glory of the sun;
Such golden, flowing motion, dipping in perilous play
Forgets the warm assurances of day.

Resistance dies, is plucked so gently from
Our paralyzed wills, we hardly know it gone.
We are surrendered to the moon:
The light compels us, pole-stars to its orbit,
We shine in darkness fixed, invisible.
Too late for the last withdrawal, we are lost
In the intricacies of yellow frost.

Fantasies in the brain, restlessness in the heart,
Desire for the unattainable, the pure romantic long-
    ing—
Ruined towers in the air, a yearning toward the sea,
For its deep death, so cool, and languorous:
These are the favorite symptoms written down;
The pressure of the moon on the rare spirit,

The wild attraction and the deep repulsion,
The irresistible compulsion.

Dogs bark invisible terror, the trees loom sharply.
These ague glamours shake down mortal ill;
The wind beloved by lunatics and lovers
Descends and sways the grass, compels the lost
Disheveled light as sharp as silver daggers,
Such light as never from Olympus poured
But dark Judean light, sorrowful, pain-extolling
And Christian light, the Gothic thunder rolling.

The Runaway

Silent and stealthy days that hour by hour
Spring up unnoticed as a flower
In summer grass; and like a breath, a light, a feather,
Make my world's weather.
I wished to weave a garland, deep and rare,
To wear upon my hair,
Or a long chain, intricate, strong, and fine,
To sound through stillness and to shine,
To bind the intangible days that so efface
Themselves with me, and run so dull a pace.
O they have run! They have gone! Nor have they set
Their seal of vast regret
Upon that wide and echoing door
That, opening, opens, shuts and sounds no more.
How to pursue Life's Runaway? Let go
The innumerable sands that through my fingers flow?
Forego the moons and waters of the mind:
Today is all that you shall find.

The Messenger

So on one night he came,
And left upon my breast
Engraved in sharpest flame
The words on which I rest.

The seasons and the sky
Grew far too still and clear
Who heard the trumpet cry
In that heroic year.

The broken bread, the wine
Whose simple mystery
Man's curious thoughts refine
Into a vaster law,
I saw.

Till the small house took light
And shone enlarged and tall
In every glittering wall
That faced the night.

For that prized messenger
Who, for a little while
Revealed his haunted face,
I write, I shape my style.

And let it be as pure
As that unearthly brow
Whose words I study now
And keep secure.

To love the truth, to shield
Its hard and lonely way,
To choose the stark defeat,
Rather than seek retreat
When it is well to yield.

The Dream

In that rich burial ground where the leveled dead
Lie darkened in extinction, I have groped
Through solitudes like death, as hopeless, lonely.
The Gothic terror in suspended air,
The cemetery reached, I saw the flowers,
Live roots among the dead, blazing in dark
Red bloom on marble, purple on the tombs,
Flushed in the light, like an expiring passion—
No ghost, no shadow stirred.
The reassuring blood raced through my veins,
Aware and deathless in the dead meadow.
Stars, thick as clustered flowers, enriched the heavens.
And light as cold as ether tinted the tombs;
But at one tomb, the light fell down aslant:
"Approach, approach, and read, and know no more."

Through creeping moss I read my name; I know
My name obscured, my tomb the smallest there.
No cypress weeps, but the moon's steady eye
Brims on it with a studied, bright compassion,
Irrevocable as the spoken word, poignant as love.

Nightpiece

Pursued by demons, he
Leaves listening trees behind;
The faintly ominous wind
Murmurs unceasingly;
He mounts his horse to ride
Out of the quick storm's reach.
Fear has a subtle speech
That is so low and kind—
A ruined angel's face
And an envenomed mind
(Death sleeps in its embrace)—

Rides fast into the wood
Where the masked stranger stood,
Feels horror in his blood
And sees cloaked misery
Point with its fleshless hand
To the infested land:
Even the smallest blade
Of shuddering new grass
Unites in powerful shade
And will not let him pass.
All night wind-furies rave
Upon the blossoming grave
Of many a murdered man,
But the remote sky sheds balm
In gentle, cloudy rain,
Slant coolness that can calm
The phantoms of his brain.
No more is he accursed
Who has endured the worst.

Oh, the sweet rain, the dew
That must foretell the morn

And heaven's earliest blue
Now under gray eclipse,
To ride for love's own sake
Into the weeping skies
Until the morning-break
Breathes coolness on his lips
And love across his eyes:
He sees the young dawn rise
Pale on her silver bed
And light as fresh as springs
From mountain watershed
Pours from her opening wings.

Cold Morning Sky

Oh, morning fresh and clear as heavenly light,
Like warmth of love within the unwilling breast,
Sad to be so possessed,
Always the delicate shafts, piercing and bright,
Troubling my rest.

Neither tempestuous now, nor tormented
As when in fragrant, unforgotten air
Of the blood's April, all the world was spent
In passionate discontent,
In rapture and despair.

But like rich gold beat thin into a thread,
Metallic-firm and shadow-fine as thought,
So this new Eros rests his shining head
Upon a book much prized and seldom read,
Glad to be captured, shielded and untaught.

Then, under morning, everlasting morning,
Clear as new joy, cool with expectant breath,
The mystery takes blood, the arriving sun gives warning;
The soul within its sheath
Explains, endures, interprets all the bliss,
Once new and unexplained;
The lucid flower is named, the numbered kiss,
The pulse-beat numbered and reduced to this
And nothing is profaned.

But airy-light, and fragile, bitter-sweet,
A small bell rings and all enchantment's done

In smallest intervals of expanding dawn;
But quiet fills the eyes, lightens the feet,
Dissolves the wonder, all fulfilled, complete.

Images in Lake Water

FOR BRYHER

The tree's sun-glittering arms are bowed
With graceful supplication in lake water.
Metallic-green and musically still
Float tree and water in one image, solitary and proud,
Till the bird-image joins them and the cloud.

Idly I watch the glimmering lights depart,
So gay falls summer glittering on the lake
And on the dreaming trees, on my transfigured heart
Grown iridescent for a shadow's sake.

Unchanging and transparent solitude
Where mobile waters haunt the enduring dream
That trembles like a lily on the stream,
A troubled whiteness on a heavy green,
A starry snowdrop on a summer scene.

Imagination colors all our watching mood,
The day contracted to a pool, a tree, a shade
All summer shining in a little space,
And the slow falling of the night delayed
With flowing images in the mind, betrayed
In mirrored silence, my unquiet face.

The Island

I sacrifice this illand unto thee
And all whom I lov'd there, and who lov'd mee.
— DONNE

I give this island green in the green sea
To underseas of floating memory,
Where all I loved and feared lie secure
In iceberg cold, jewel-frozen, diamond-pure.
There once a boat with Christ's own banners set
Rose from a mist of cloudy-violet-jet
Against blue mountain-tops, and cold inhuman
Came from the shore the wails of ancient women.
Descend like that old saint, patrician, wise
Driving the evil serpents with your eyes
Descend like him to aboriginal dark
And on the heart of evil set your mark,
Green-growing trefoil of immortal love,
See the black ravens scattered, and your dove
Garlanded with the sacred mistletoe
While the druid voices rise in anger, grow
Until the Latin music drowns the sound.

The sacred maidens dance nor touch the ground,
So light, so vibrant, so ethereally,
Rose-petals blown upon an angry sea.
This land remembers, must forever hold
Music of wind-wet silver, and that sense
Of low, subdued, and secret violence.
And the shawled women praying, the bare feet
The green-eyed children, ruddy, ragged, fleet;
The emerald waters sheeted in green glass,
The hills of shaded violet, green-black grass
And the faint odor of dissolving snow
When first the young buds on the blackthorn blow.

This aboriginal landscape, primitive,
Drives me far westward where I cannot live:
Oh, to the warmer, gentler, happier South
My soul draws closer, to relieve its drouth,
Not this lost isle, this West that leans to North.
Can I survive? I send this message forth
To you, the bravest of survivors: Look and lean
From your high tower of vision, all is green,
This land is in your blood, you will prefer
To be this chill's, this mist's, interpreter.

The Daisy

Having so rich a treasury, so fine a hoard
Of beauty water-bright before my eyes,
I plucked the daisy only, simple and white
In its fringed frock and brooch of innocent gold.

So is all equilibrium restored:
I leave the noontide wealth of richer bloom
To the destroyer, the impatient ravisher;
The intemperate bee, the immoderate bird.

Of all this beauty felt and seen and heard
I can be frugal and devout and plain,
Deprived so long of light and air and grass,
The shyest flower is sweetest to uncover.

How poor I was: and yet no richer lover
Discovered joy so deep in earth and water;
And in the air that fades from blue to pearl,
And in a flower white-frocked like my small daughter.

Lullaby

Ruin falls on blackening skies
And disaster lies in wait
For the heart and for the state;
Loud the voices in the street
Shout unhealing remedies.

Sleep, beloved, while you may:
Heralds of the Augustan day
That arise as you awake
Can consume but never slake
The strong thirst, intense and deep,
For the peace that need not sleep.

Let the lion have his hour,
Let the evil beasts devour
Leaf and vine and fruit and flower;
Theirs the night but yours the time
Known to the Vergilian clime
When the ancient world, distressed,
Found peace in an infant's breast.

Still remote and gay and young
Sing the stars in ancient peace,
Heralding the great release
In their wordless tongue.
Close your eyes and let them sing
In the morning that will bring
What strange beasts to haunt the spheres?
Revelations? New-found fears?

Let the old world fall away
As the great beasts leave their prey;

Let the dogs and cats destroy
That which they cannot enjoy.
New as life and death and sleep
Shall the cyclic rivers creep,
Bringing learning, art, and thought
New again to be renewed,
Revived, restored, and still uncaught,
The intangible pursued.

Sleep, beloved, in the changes
Light from bright to darkness ranges:
Venus, ocean-young, arises,
Love again the earth surprises
Naked, dreaming, peaceful, free,
Springing from the bitter sea
Of unending destiny.

Midsummer Noon

Calm, ripe, and gold the shadows fell
On trees whose green was feather-light
In the sweet air against a sky
Tranced in the rich midsummer spell
Of beauty, warm, compacted, bright,
Glowing in clear intensity.

And in my wrist, and at my brain,
The jeweled tick of time and sun
Subsided and grew still again.
I saw the sparkling shadows run
Through glimmering avenues of trees
To exquisite oblivion;
And the high pitch of noon was done.

And in my head, my ears, my heart
And in the subtle wrist-pulse clear
I felt a heavy faintness start;
In intimate and desperate fear
Death's elegant, worn face drew near.

The dwindling shadow of that high
Perfection that had grown complete,
Had drained my joy's deep fountains dry
And left things salt that once were sweet.

The world through shadow softly glowing
Restored itself through alien eyes
Restored its lowered love and heat
Into the sun-dilated eyes
And natural quiet softly blowing
Descended on the ripening wheat.

Rare Joy

Not plucked like stars, flowers from the sky,
Are you, rare joy whose artless glance
Makes light and sweet the lover's cry,
Teaches the withered heart to dance,
Lights the glazed eyeballs of the blind,
And pours its healing on the mind.

Rare as the tropic birds of light
In northern islands dull with frost
Are you, restorer of true sight
And that first early freshness lost
Through troubled years; that goodness caught
In innocence, now always sought.

Crown with white violets the hour
When the clock's pulse grows faint with care,
When beauty weeps within her bower
And sees the fatal, first, gray hair
Among her golden tresses show
And feels time's dimming afterglow.

Dear as an infant's face, as loved
As youngest child, by its fond mother
Outstretch your happy hand ungloved,
Soft flesh to awakened flesh, no other
Can stir the arid roots of time
In a perpetual summer clime.

None, none like you, dear joy, can move
The eyes to sun, the limbs to speed
In the quick harmony of love
When anger makes the silence bleed.
Teach, teach, your scholar how to send
The message that seals friend to friend.

Water and Shadow

(After Sir Philip Sidney)

By the long flow of green and silver water
Rushing in limpid light from savage mountains
I walked beneath the shadow of the mountains
That dimmed with barbaric dark, light-jeweled waters.

Grandeur and majesty and strength descended
On my right hand and left, in tones of liquid laughter
Sweeter than airy birds, child-laughter, star-descended,
Star-pointed joy like children's eyes in laughter.

Ran the bright waters down the savage breast
Of the great mountains, sweetness from the strong
Melting the somber stone with fountained beauty—
Young, sparkling, dancing on the frowning mountains.

And from the mirror of the divided skies,
As if flashed from the sun on golden streamers,
A child descended, small hands bright with flowers,
The sun-sheen gold on her hair, stars on her azure frock.

Between the night and bright, the delicate and stark,
She flew to earth, scattering flowers and singing
Always of the long flow of green and silver water
And the barbaric shadow of the mountains.

Spring Morning

The arrowy gold whose winter span
Of life was lost in wind and water
Shed from the sky, to waters ran
Casting new life upon the water.

From water Love herself arose,
Limbs laved in seawater and sun;
Again her smile dissolves the snow,
Hearts bared to flowering of the sun.

O, brief and glittering time of joy
When the long thoughts of youth run free
And garlanded the girl and boy
With the young flowers as bright and free:

The dark head and the golden one
Glad in the sun, rose-garlanded
Dream of adventures in the sun,
High actions, proud, rose-garlanded;

And from their dreams the laurel grows
While artlessly the tide of love
Circles, expands, contracts, and grows
Through sunlit avenues of love.

The Greek, the natural feet of dawn
Wade in lake waters, calm the sea;
Her footsteps, light on the green lawn,
Sound like faint signals from the sea.

Gold-streaked the air in luminous flashes,
Shadows of trees in water flowing,
Nostalgic tears on awakened lashes
Remember joy, its ebbing, flowing.

FROM *The Listening Landscape*

1941

The Descent of the Vulture

As he left the ship he saw this, only this
Painted in clear vision on the sunny air:
That it was pleasant and green on *terra firma* there,
But he heard a vulture scream over an abyss.

Green, smiling, solid the earth; the dazzling sky
Ripe for adventure, spilling good nature down;
Fortuna the giddy goddess in her flashing golden gown,
Distributing joy, fame, honors, and prosperity.

Adorable as always, her eyes seemed cooler, narrow,
As if too full of knowledge and desire,
And with slow, decorous steps she walked through a
        cloud of fire,
Smiling as the vulture devoured a sparrow.

Gallant, alert, erect, he surveyed the dangerous strand,
Kissed his hand to the goddess who looked farewell;
Lightning flashed, and thunder pealed like a bell, like a
        knell—
He was left forever in the fatal land.

Where neither beauty, presence, nor wit can bless
Nor intellect, affection, charm, prevail—
He saw the river dim, the crags darken, the last boat sail,
And the pleasant land become a wilderness.

The listening landscape heard but did not say
That the armed antagonists were waiting behind the tree,

Dark spreading tree, emblem of life and destiny
Under your shade no leaves dance, no nymphs play.

For warm flesh cannot compete with grass and stone,
Nor the bright face conquer against a world in arms;
All his adventure is done, but the fruitful sleepy farms,
Slumber in moonlight, till the evil bird has flown.

The Seance

When will that voice come? Drawn from the air in that
    drab room,
The plain table, the yellow curtains slowly fading,
The bare stone floor,
Wind on the roof mocking the spirit's gloom,
A knocking at the mind's door.

O but that Voice arrived marvelous, young, and gay,
Death shaking the young spirit loose
From the corruptions of the grave
Had shed his soul on ever-widening day,
The luminous body rising from decay.

Now by the wound still marked on the quieted breast,
Agony, defeat, despair, each grief defied, checked,
Tell how the iron gates sound,
In that vast netherworld whose meanings unexpressed
Grew candid, clear, direct.

Century after century of silence, war upon war,
Since in the autumn on a noonstruck hill
Your brief and brilliant years were told
And the slow, oncoming sea
Drew in that scarlet and that gold.

"Say that the early dead mature, in the dark, the mold,
Grow ripe in ungathered powers, sleep in rich chastity
(In that fruitful bed). Whose children never born
Haunt us in visions of eternity,
Perceptive, delicate, and cold.

"Say that short-lived Beauty is a stronger force than death:
Complex among the simple elements,
It long survives the fiercer, brutal dead;

Charm, grace, and sweetness draw an enduring breath,
Their smiling spell, sky-drawn, tranced, overhead."

These things the exquisite lost Voice once said to me,
Till the plain table glowed with sun, the curtains shone
With faith's fine texture of light,
The floors rain-washed in cool serenity,
Reflecting spirit eyes, withdrawn and bright.

House of Chimeras

Always when the door opened such surprise
Clouded imagination; when we walked
Through the long drawing room the summer seemed to fall
With a quick shimmer on the ground

And stained the wine-gold carpets, colored our fear
With chimeras and delusions; in that world
Only the life-sized portraits on the wall
Glowed in fantastic life forever clutching roses.

We always looked for a sign, for a word, for a banner,
For a god's name in whose great sign we conquer,
But nothing seemed to answer, no one at all,
Though One sat in the room forever writing letters.

Nervous, distraught, the pure profile, the priceless pearls
Pale on her pale satin, pale against dark eyes
Breathing awhile, watching the long days fall
From the long windows to a sleepless sea.

The amazing letters! sealed, signed, posted,
Sent to what destination? what far country?
We never asked. Noon cast a silver pall
Over the hours, night always found us waiting

For the white daisy fields to shine, for the wild rose
To open and expose its heart of gold.

In morning light small rivers seemed to call
In spinet music toward a rushing water.

And always voices silenced suddenly
In the long corridors near the marble fountains,
The garden voices of hope in every hall,
The male, the female voices, hushed and homesick.

Face at the Window

Who calls aloud through rainy skies?
That face on whose long eyelash dries
The unfalling tear? I see you rise
From sullen heavens gray and dull.
You follow me when I would turn,
Fly and escape. Avert my head,
Still you pursue me, tormented.

When shall the warm love glow and pour
Its richest sunlight through the mind?
Between us glassy walls that blind,
Air's healing vision, and a door,
Frail as a summer's day, as strong:
"The summers of Hesperides are long."

Long, deep, intangible, and strange,
As heavy jungles unexplored,
Encircled as the world I range,
When shall the natural rain and sun
Deliver me? and be restored
The lucid, calm, autumnal plain?

Through window glass your image calls
And with the rain my own tear falls,
Remembers, halts, recalls, recalls
That summer land, that tree of air
Upon a world of brightness sought,
The golden apples shining there,
Eternal, falling, never caught.

There we have squandered richness, powers,
Kindness that will not come again;
There painted warriors, tigers, flowers
Blaze on each roofless house for token,
There the gold pitcher falls, lost, broken;
Tarnished lies the silver bowl.

The Renunciation

And you leaned against the door and breathed
Sharply as if to escape your own heart's beat
Quickly, as if undone, as if an assassin's feet
Moved through the noonday heat,

And a young girl, swift-footed, flower-wreathed
Parted the branches, ran to your side, and you unheeding
Never saw the invisible wound in her heart, quietly bleeding:

The open door, inviting, pleading, threatening—
You saw the aging furniture, felt the heavy air,
The comforting presence of each familiar thing
Nor saw how she grew tall and tall, still standing there.

Grew to your fear's height, or how remorselessly,
She unbound the full glory of her burning hair,
Made taut your hunted heart's anxiety,
While an old conflict left you helpless there.

Between the comfortable familiar house
And the twisted road from which you always fled
Because of the wild beauty that it shed,
From high autumnal heavens forever yellow and red,

And because your throat was frozen, your tongue dry,
You could not summon the passionate words, you said
Only what could be passed from eye to eye,
Less than a breath, less than a sigh.

Always the door closes, you despair and fly
Toward the full memory and the compelling tide,
And return to the loathed room in desire, disdain, and pride—

Lost between love and dread, the unreturning cry.

Lightning for Atmosphere

The warriors, tigers, flowers of Delacroix
Painted upon the walls ablaze with light,
Pure light, cloud-blanched, that unstained white,
Queen of the colors, whom all other tints destroy,
Color of the dwindling moon.

Or white lightning, seascapes of Châteaubriand,
Shores the dramatic ocean beats upon,
Where the lone hero, gloomy on the wild strand
Sees friends and lovers and companions gone,
Hawk, gull, and heron flying.

White-capped mountains, peaks of dazzling snow,
Cloud-pointed Alps, sharp unclimbable heights,
Burning effulgence of the northern lights
Toward whose clear radiance our desire grows,
White heat of the infinite.

The intense young lady seen in a dream long gone,
Ringleted, lonely in her villa by the sea,
Peers through a misted window, sees the floating swan;
Wild geese whiten the sky, lighten the fir tree
Shrill, sound-shattering solitude.

White-gowned in the thin, nocturnal air,
She throws her book aside and her fine ear
Hears flying catches of joy, the ecstatic fear,
Whiteness of the abyss; through her soul's precipice
Dark flows the midnight of her hanging hair.

She, through a deep hallucination seeing
Strong waves from sheer, salt oceans, drowned lovers
Pallid and proud. The white blank mind discovers

Figures rising from waterfalls, appearing, fleeing
Into damp creeks, into the steep ravines.

All hearts have their precipices, Alps, white peaks,
Moments when the white bird with the deep wound must
    come
To sing and swoon upon enchanted willows;
The heart disguises its symbols, peers through the hid
    ravines
Steep-gaping between wars.

The Listening Landscape

Now the children are asleep
Night uncharts its diagram;
In the suburbs women weep
And no hero comforts them.
Now the prophecies come true
That the cards and stars foretold
And the reckoning is due
And the sun is lunar-cold.

Innocence and Justice wait
At the moldy, opening door
Carved with fabled beasts, and Hate
Takes its station at the gate.
Presenting arms the sentinels
March to guard the sleeping land
Mustered from their several hells,
The mute, rebellious angels stand.

Evening stupor, slyly mad,
Corrodes the heart, engenders truth,
Exploits the nightmares you have had,
Reveals the errors of your youth.
You shall see the pointed finger
Mark you out from other men
And the pin-prick wound will linger
Never to be healed again.

Hide no secrets now, for all,
All must be revealed and told
As the bells of judgment call
Melancholy, stern, and cold.
Hearing them the children wake,
At the sound Love's eyes grow dark,

In each flower a sleeping snake
And the arrows pierce the mark.

All, all shall learn the secret hid
In your secluded rooms, shall know
The name, the hour, and what you did
And where your private gardens blow.
And the Recording Judge marks down,
The buried fear, the hidden sigh,
Exposed to all the prying town—
What saps your strength, what drains
     your warm blood dry!

The False Summer

It might have been in the heart of a deep forest,
So wide the shade, dense-thicketed where only a pool's sound
Strikes—dancing over stones, with a sound cool and airy,
But it was in a city park, enclosed from the stone street
By an iron gate,
By a phalanx of trees.

We followed a thin stream of rumor, were led to a trail
Of unwinding memory, pounding and low like a moving sea
Till we came to a hot meadow; then one voice pastoral-muted
Pealed through the air like a silver bell and sang like an
      angel;
It drew rain from the heavens,
Bowed the trembling trees.

By a glint of gold through the trees, we traced the falling hair
Of Amaryllis; she who lives in that burning meadow,
Whose voice as cool as a stream calms the false summer,
Who points to a mirage of streams when the soul faints
      with heat,
She who when wheels are turning calls to the pastoral land,
Sings of eternal silence,
Cool grass and tree-arched groves.

Voice of delight and fear to the lost, listening children!
They run for home, they gather their toys, the nursemaids
      call,
And suddenly rivers of blood ran on and on as always,
The nursemaids wept for their old country, green in the
      angry sea,
While the heavenly voice kept singing
In the green solitude.

We too remembered the flag at half-mast, the crumbling
    fortress,
In that old country where we fled to danger
Because the ruins were lovely, because Death wore an
    angel's mask,
We saw how the blood-rivers followed, stained the secure
    landscape
Even in that rich, round song
The frozen fear, the warning.

We are lost if the iron gate closes, if the intricate thickets
Draw us deep in delightful shade, toward the charmed
    singing,
Green song and deep, sharp, pure and steep, clean, green,
Song heard in the opening leaves, the closing flowers,
Do not detain us
Lest you forever claim us.

Amaryllis who sings in the shade till the storm leaps and
    gathers,
Till the invaders march through the streets sealing the
    fountains,
Poisoning the springs of life, destroying our secret shelters,
Drawing us further from home till we stand on the enemy
    street;
And the uneasy charm is broken,
The angel music from a demon's throat.

Girl's Song

And always through my window pane
The shadow of a fine horseman riding
Over the dry plain.
Though in my heart it is green summer
I live in blossoming days
Always and always.

When will you descend,
Gay, smiling rider?
Delightful enemy, long-promised friend,
Spring from your saddle, moving toward my heart
Intent on murder or a kiss?
Here in the light I stand,
All summer in my hand.

My season sways with light,
Life streams from my round eyes,
Dreams with impassioned sight
See how the ripening fields remember me;
My feet are planted in full noon,
My words will blossom soon.

Though now they lie within my breast,
Heavy and dormant, shy and shivering
With what is unexpressed,
Soon they will melt the frozen throat in song
And locked rivers open, run
In the full mid-day sun.

The Casket of Pandora

When for a long time I contemplate this box
Carved so cunningly by the hand of a god,
Glittering with withheld treasure,

I take no delight in my eye's light, the body's pleasure.

How many times awake, or in sleep, a voice
Through the open window, from the earth or the shore,
Says, "This thing, this thing, you must not explore."

The shade of evil falls on the pure grass;
It shoots up from my life's root, its face
Troubling the emptiness of clear water.

And somewhere in my dream, the sound of pain and
    slaughter.

Then waking in my room, the casket gleams;
The maiden pallor of the morning light
Pierces my heart with an unnatural night

For in my world it is always morning;
The dew refreshes the mind, the early flowers
Hint of a delicate spring, foretell a green summer.

Now always at my door, the step of a newcomer

Whose face I never see though I open the door,
Though I look through sun-struck windows,
Though I peer through the enchanted dawn.

Then I touch the casket's lid, jewel-bright as dew on
    the lawn,

Locked, locked as a scent in a closed flower's heart.
O, to open the glittering box, to shut my ears
To the small voice that seems to sound from a tree.

Through my window the tree takes shape, has a face I
    cannot see;

High, marvelous tree! half-sun, half, wine-dark.
I feel the murmur run through your sap like blood
Eager for the deed to be done, wild to be understood!

Head of Medusa

How long she waited for her executioner!
She who froze life to stone, whose hissing hair
Once grew as waved and flowing as the sea,
Ash-damp and dreadful now. The fabulous mystery,
    the shame,
Forever in that cave where man nor beast came,

Came and returned to life; so great the curse
Of the invulnerable enemy whose eyes immerse
Medusa's soul in this foul universe,
Turns her warm body passionate, fleshed with fire,
Into this loathsome thing no men desire.

Cast in the final loneliness she must lie,
Knowing that all who look on her will die
(The savage sorrow frozen in her sigh)—
Even as she meets the look of fear and hate
Their blood dries and their flesh must expiate.

But now her Perseus comes, foe or deliverer?
Bringing the welcome end. For whom her serpents stir,
Brute force and animal terror, the soul's tormentor
Subside; low-water calm, slow, unperceptively
Comes he who sets her free.

And now the end nears. Through steelpoint warm blood
Shall flow in purification. Her world made clean and
    good,
Through pain the Immortal's hatred is withstood.
Even now in the gold shield
One faces her, his life-blood uncongealed,

Prepares for the quick stroke that sets her free
From the cold terror in all eyes that see.
Even now the slayer's hand displays the mystery
That once vainglorious and guilty head,
Emptied of all its sorrow and its dread!

Interview in Midsummer

Deep were the woods and the birdsong
Was oversweet and overlong;
The river tumbled through stoneways,
The long ferns dipped in dew would gaze
At my reflection in the pool
Unquiet, distracted, never cool,
Whitening like them through widening glass
At what was coming and would pass
Between us and the genial sun
When the midsummer day was done.

Yet happy, happy, was the time
Of liquid golden air, the clime
Of ease and joy and wildflower grace,
Of singing trees and cobweb lace,
Daisy and fragile buttercup,
Gay, slight-stemmed heads held lightly up,
Bowing and dancing in the wood,
Wraiths of the whispering solitude.

Now riding slowly through the gleam,
The stranger came—face seen in dream
Under the slim and sweeping willow,
Or troubled sleep on the hard pillow,
With no surprise, with no alarms,
I knew that face; oft in my arms
Have seen that graceful form, that head,
Nightlong on the destined bed.

His face and eyes and form behold
That at the appointed station told
The hereditary enemy—
That veiled but known identity;

In the long-sought-for stranger, trace
(Even while locked in his embrace)
Shadows of warning and distress
In the warm smile, the light caress.

Then ancient sadness dark and still
Put out the brightness, long and chill
Sweet, sharp, and cold, the nightfires leap
From smoldering chasms old and steep
As if a fiery spirit hid,
Its bright eyes through a coffin lid
Blazing through steel and wood and stone,
And made their restless vision known.

The wild air thickened as I stood,
Trembling in the silenced wood;
The voice, form, eyes encompassed me
In sadness and intensity;
Before I felt his pallor flow
Into my veins, I named my foe
Nor did love lessen, nor the pain
Nor did I wish my life again.

Girl with the Golden Bough

Because it was their spirit's sunny season,
The virgin year flushed warm with faith.
They held a golden branch, dispelled the wraith
That spoke of age and reason.

Hyacinth and violet-wreaths their only ornament,
They wear the heaven blue, the purple paled to white
Girls whom the Sun-God gives (being of his stem and
    true descent)
The secret of all music and delight.

O but the fair-haired archer smiling with love
Has chosen one; in her his knowledge gleams;
The milk and honey of his beauty streams
Into her blood, power and strength from above.

And toward the Sun she moves where none can follow,
Tracing with golden bough the migrating soul
Where sacred maidens dance, each with a silver bowl
Toward Dionysus or Apollo.

Falling Tears, Awakening Heavens

Tears from awakening heavens, flowing suddenly, silently—
The great stream that Saint Augustine saw as a limitless sea:

When he awoke in silence and joy seeing his tempters depart,
Tears from awakening heavens, melting the hardened heart;

From heaven's wide opening eye, quietly night and day
Dropped the great tears that washed all guilt away.

Intellectual pride that sought a god's ascension,
Spiritual pride that fed on error and dissension.

This I beheld attempting to fly from my Friend,
Ran from him; dived; sought world's end; found no end.

From memory that found no change, no shadow of turning,
Smoldering like a great torch, a flame perpetually burning,

Tears from Memory falling into a boundless sea,
Recall the time I have wasted, how time has wasted me.

Mine was an earth of thistles, sharp to the stranger hand,
Harsh to the naked feet of the alien in my land.

I hear the invader's tread; I await the trespasser,
Hear through weeping heavens the dark-drenched grasses
        stir.

Hate was the world's color, anger the poet's theme
Even with the wise and gentle; love, like a rose on the stream
Floating unpetaled, ignored, as if in a sorrowful dream.

See how my stubborn thistles harsh in the mid-day
Bow in the melting heavens, stoop and are washed away;

I leave to the growing children this empty field and clean.
When will they plant it forever with grass fresh-sown and
    green?
Or the tamed doe leap where the lion has been?

Child in the Crystal

Through the world's low-water, the turn of the year,
He shines through crystal, rosy-tinctured, clear;
His soul is lit
In that white flame by which the round earth spins.

All joy and sorrow, hope, fear, enmity,
All daysprings of desire run to a kindred sea,
But he enclosed in glass
Reveals his beauty like a field of flowers.

The heavens star-slit, expose that auroral sky
Where the desires long sleeping, wake and sigh;
The infant Time
Speaks of dewspangled lawns, of lutes tuned to the wind's
     voice.

Seen only as a face reflected in crisped and turning air,
His lustre enriches the summer, his small hand dimpled
     bare,
Touches the sybilline leaves
And in the wind, the prophetic books are scattered.

Of his voice, breath, essence, grace, an image grows,
Ripens like yellow light, expands into rising suns,
Angel of harmony
In whose small heart the eternal clockbeat ticks.

Counting the unborn hours, the opening regions of joy,
Fire-flash on fine-webbed clouds, the imprisoned boy
Sparkles—till bells
Of delight, timbred with fire, accent the declining day.

Thy Sire is manifest through fire, but Thou in the fire's
     light;

Thy great descent is made clear in the dews and stars of
  the night,
Thy beauty brief and dear,
Quicksilver in water, ecstasy pointing to dark, in rust and
  smoke.

Nor forget thy Mother whose garlanded locks still shine,
Love's image smiling from her house to thine,
O till the crystal break
See how desire strikes fire, draws life from that element.

Children of the Island

And one brief season is their only year,
Summer illumines all and is their year.
Soon at the rumored breath of cold they fade
Into fine air of which their breath is made.

Long have I wandered, seeking, seeking them
Who are my spirit's roots, the flower, the stem;
Only in startled glimpses in a dream
Their white, their gold, their coral, gleam,

Islanded in the sun, then disappear,
Since one brief season is their only year;
Lost as the wildrose in the long grass,
Their half-seen images through watery glass.

Vision of childhood in the aging world
So soon decays, so fades, the morning world;
The child face printed on the mother's heart,
The visions seen in flight and start.

For one brief season is their only year,
When sunken islands from the sea appear,
Crowned with deep light the childish forms arise
Bringing renewal to our drowsy eyes.

That laughter, softness, sweetness and surprise,
Bright as elusive air from Paradise
When swept by Time's long wave we drift far, far,
From where the children of the island are.

The Golden Rose

FOR RUTH PITTER

A flower that in eternal summer blows
Fairer than Waller's rose, or his who sung
(Ausonius!) the newblown golden rose,
Like Ronsard's rose, or Herrick's it has sprung,

Breathes for a while to hearts that feel and know
How slow upon the lyric, joyous lark,
Warm in the Latin heaven's afterglow,
Fell the barbarian cloud, the angry dark.

When fountains of despair run dry, when chance,
War, ruin, misery, their cycles round,
Men turn again to music, sun, and dance,
The burning roses on the classic ground.

The Interpreter of Silence

And thou shalt be brought down, and shalt speak out of the ground, and thy speech shall be low out of the dust, and thy voice shall be as one that hath a familiar spirit out of the ground, and thy speech shall whisper out of the dust.
                                                    —ISAIAH 29

Isolation is populous, it has many voices
Shrill-sounding, fern-fine; silence has many faces,
Thin-eared, has sensitive long hands, is delicate in choices.

It preys on the deserted lawn, the suburban summer;
Waits for the feet that must come, that never come,
The familiar tread of the awaited guest, the startling new-
    comer.

The pink and white magnolia tree is stirred
By rumors of one who comes to pluck her blossoms;
It questions the breeze, it shakes at the sound of a bird.

Meanwhile the watching windows facing streams,
Reflect the nervous air, thin glass on watery grass,
They dream of the sun's power, his strength, his life-
    compelling beams.

The sensitive children play fresh-voiced as fountains;
Their arms are full of flowers; they are always singing,
It is not for them that we wait; they fly as birds to the moun-
    tains.

Why do you wait? for whom do you pray? whose hidden
    voice divining
The Prince of the Host of the Air, mailed angel, mighty
    cherubim
Who comes as a thief in the night, star-sprayed water-
    streaming?

From the stone towers of Assyria, mounted on the sun's
      horse,
He shall speak the word that shall splinter the night,
He will set the bushes afire, divert the swift stream from its
      course.

The interpreter of silence, the consoler of patient pain,
Who arrives in unguarded quiet, dismounts, knocks at the
      gate,
For whom the magnolia listens, for whom the children sing
      and wait.

The White Dress

Imperceptively the world became haunted by her white dress.
Walking in forest or garden, he would start to see
Her flying form; sudden, swift, brief as a caress,
The flash of her white dress against a darkening tree.

And with forced unconcern, withheld desire, and pain
He beheld her at night; and when sleepless in his bed,
Her light footfalls seemed loud as cymbals; deep as his disdain,
Her whiteness entered his heart, flowed through from feet to head.

Or it was her face at a window, her swift knock at the door,
Then she appeared in her white dress, her face as white as her
     gown;
Like snow in midsummer she came and left the rich day poor;
And the sun chilled and grew higher, remote, and the moon
     slipped down.

So the years passed; more fierce in pursuit her image grew;
She became the dream abjured, the ill uncured, the deed undone,
The life one never lived, the answer one never knew,
Till the white shadow swayed the moon, stayed the expiring sun;

Until at his life's end, the shadow of the white face, the white
     dress
Became his inmost thought, his private wound, the word un-
     spoken,
All that he cherished in failure, all that had failed his success;
She became the crystal orb, half-seen, untouched, unbroken.

There on his death bed, kneeling at the bed's foot, he trembling
     saw
The image of the Mother-Goddess, enormous, archaic, cruel,
Overpowering the universe, creating her own inexorable law,
Molded of stone, but her fire and ice flooded the room like a pool.

And she was the shadow in the white dress, no longer slight and
     flying,
But solid as death. Her cold, firm, downward look
Brought close to the dissolving mind the marvelous act of dying,
And on her lap, the clasped, closed, iron book.

Forest of Arden

Expectant, hushed the air. Sounds heard when the earthly
    ear
Unlocks to immortal sound. Here the unsleeping dead
Sent early to the dark seek out the sun,
Walk invisibly in the living solitude.
Whitely the spirit smolders through the bone
When skeleton clean and clear the bodies shine
And move with the linear purity of a frieze.
They part the airy trees. Invisible in the thick forest,
Each one a multitude, each one alone.

What fruits does this land offer? what pleasures will it
    yield?
Fulfillment of what unobtainable joy? It is not barren
But waits behind tangible worlds. Here the spent minds
    restore
The final meaning to the relinquished shore,
Recall the scattered lives that inward, downward flow;
Time shrinks, long grasses deepen and grow.

And wait, watch the consuming solitude that lifts
The body down and seaward buoys up the spirit, flies
To dream-drenched forests, shows you their wonders.
Here is the jewel-capped snake whose lust never dies,
Ambition, power, and pride, the desire of the eye and the
    mind,
Insatiate, unquiet, it moves; its secret anger wakes
The mysterious powers of the dead that pierce the living.

The Thread of Ariadne

It leads to a light first, faint as a candle spark,
Bright welcome! when victorious from the grave
You arrive, flushed with conquest of the dark,
Glad for the sun, and my white body glowing.

Under the tree of life, where the branched beauty flames
In tapers of joy, a timeless candelabrum,
Love haloes my hair, makes daystars of my eyes—
Soon I shall find a diadem in the skies.

Only to you I bare my world, reveal, discover
How purple-rich, how ivory-white it is;
Even now my hyacinths bloom, the tall, the slight narcissi
To your withdrawn mind, my April thought bestows.

And you alert for danger, go where gaudier grows
The lip-red poppy scenting earth with sleep,
The yellow rose that leaves no scent behind,
Dreaming of perils past, and the foe, aware, unsleeping.

Wade under the full moon where the cold tide creeping
Into your vigilant blood tells of another bride,
Of a new kingdom, changing destiny, a greater cause
Of gods and heroes active at your side.

Snowstorm in January

Calm is the season, cold and clear the air,
Deep cold by which the dreaming blood is stung,
Heightened to clarity and made aware
Of the dark skeleton of trees and houses stripped of
     sun,
Grass chilled by snowcalm air, and gray quiet every-
     where.

In other lands in mirrors of ice, I saw
The ancient winter of the soul, and magnified,
Hectic, ablaze, and glittering without flaw
That burning town from which all warmth had died,
While ivory pure and linear black and white
Beneath an everlasting winter night
Shone every January branch, each icy spellbound thing
Calm, calm, as on a summer evening.

Clear whiteness brighter than the sun's warm bronze,
Swan-feathered snow! chained landscape taut and light
All richness covered now and grown austere,
As the chilled earth unfolds to deepening sight;
Then warning, premonition, and restraint,
Acceptance, resignation, and the fleet
Naked footfalls of joy, forever flying,
Till the dawn break and frozen fears depart,
Endure the silences, closed winter heart.

March Morning

Gray air flooded with gold
Pierced by the awakened wind
So clean and sharp and cold.

The mind's, the heart's best weather
Is on my world today,
The clear light, the spirit's holiday.

Again my days are told
In hope's white clarity
I feel the rose unfold

Its immemorial bliss
Rich with all memories
The warmth, the love, the kiss.

The blood's stilled rivers run
The renewed energies,
And once again the sun!

FROM *The Golden Mirror*

1944

Thou Knowest Not into
What Dreams Thou Wanderest

High have I wandered far
Beyond the imagined peak,
Ah, foolish traveler,
Pursuing such a star!

I reached the black-veined hill—
And looking deep below,
Saw savage waters spill
Foam-wreaths of snow.

Foam-wreaths that fade and gleam,
I felt my spirit drift
Under some ancient stream
Dream-deep river-swift.

Into what steeps I fall,
Through what prenatal clime
Where outcast angels call
The end of time.

How have I stumbled on,
This close, this deep distress,
This war, this marathon,
This last duress.

How innocently begun!
How childlike, ignorant,
Hoping to reach the sun,
Walk where the stars went.

Looked deep into an abyss
Of vision and despair,

Saw through a wilderness
The blessed at their prayer.

Surprised they rise, enfold
A dream-strong ambuscade
Of blue and emerald,
My soul waylayed.

Nor know now if accursed
I am, if damned, if blessed,
But burn with endless thirst.

*"Thou knowest not into what dreams thou
wanderest."*

Woman at the Piano

Rippling in the ocean of that darkening room—
The music poured from the thin hands, widening, gather-
    ing
The floods of descending night, flying from the keys
The sound of memory, then the woman singing
Vibrant and full, the resonant echoes scattered
Into a stranger's language, into a foreign country.

The rococo clock on the mantel strikes out its chimes;
The dark wind sighing through the open windows
Sends in its signals, wishes, memories;
The withdrawn room grows immense with hallucina-
    tion—
Clear woman's voice, long fingers whitely straying
Over the speaking keys, do you hear the answer?
Will the male voice answer? stirring through the walls
Behind the rustling curtains, in the declining light,
Another voice still silent seems to tremble.

Patience is all. Unloved, unlovable, lonely,
It sits on the neglected sofa, watches the fingers
Draw out the difficult music, hears the finale
Shatter the torpor of the dying room.
Now the trees through open windows aspire and flame,
Now there are footsteps, echoes, reveries—
Now two voices sound in the room where only one
Wove intricate sweetness from the simple keys;
Two voices ring in the dawn, the morning enters.

Luna and Leopardi

At the world's turning, at the hour of darkness,
When through the open window slowly rising
The full and beautiful moon poured lucid light
(O subdued gentleness of dying things)
Streaming into the room, shaking with nervous quiet
On empty tables and through trembling curtains
On the dark, steady floor:

Antique image of Luna, pale, full-breasted virgin,
Your glittering shafts of gold pierced every window,
Entered the heart where dark and longing mingled,
Entered the avid brain and left its wound,
Invisible, never bleeding, dulled with pain,
Asking the unspoken question never answered,
"Are you alive? How long have you been buried?"

A dog barked. The voice of Daphne sighing in the laurel
Answered his harsher with a softer tone,
And both implored the night in love and pity,
"Divine satellite of day, pale-shining Luna,
Ambassadress-companion of the Sun,
Assure us of your favor and compassion."

And she rising from her bed of clouds—
Languid and ailing in the waning world—
Spoke in her voiceless speech through moving stars,
"Never shall you have a cry of love from me,
Nor from the generative earth, nor from the Sun,
The understanding-uncompassionate.

"The majesty of human suffering
I can revere who, burning like the Sun,
Chill like man's age or girl's voice in the tree,
Or change from form to form like the Great Mother

Who mirrors in each form the changing world,
The fire, the water, and the blood.

"I, Luna, too, reflect the shifting world,
The virgin image of the indifferent Mother,
I, too, can nourish life, am served by eunuchs,
The soldier virile in his death, the panting steed,
The firm-eyed serpent and the gentle deer,
The imagined phoenix and the unicorn."

Then in the darkness in the thoughtful evening,
All questions died into a various query,
"Are you alive?" or, *"Can you face the Sun?"*
Know that the hour grows late, the reprieve uncoming,
The guards are waiting at the threshold of the Sun.
Can you endure the silence of that silver bed?
Enormous in the caverns of the Moon,
Far, far, from all the pleasures of the Sun?

Death and Transfiguration

When that body loved
As no other was
Withered into the grass
And all tears were shed,
A dark tree at your head,
And at your feet,
A cold stone
Recording your defeat,

The soul rose from the sod,
And sang alone
Praise to its God
In full-voiced glory
And the scattered bones flew,
Assembled and complete.
Again that sweetness ran
Into a living man.

Then *Gloria Domine!*
To Him who will not let
The reluctant heart forget
The silver and the gold
That dropped into the mold,
Who bids the high sun stand
At His uplifted hand,
Who makes a poem of praise
Out of your broken days;

Who lets no beauty sink
Beyond recall,
Who feels all tears that fall,
Who stands at Terror's brink

And shields the sparrow's wing
From the last sting.

Rise, gentle soul, relate
What few believe or see:
How through harsh paths and strait
You fell to victory;
In love's house none are lost,
No suffering vain;
Death purchased at such cost
Buys life again.

Variations on a Theme by George Herbert

After so many deaths to breathe again,
To see the clouded windows open, brighten
With recovered sight. To see the blackness whiten
And fountained love gush from the arid plain.

"After so many deaths to live and write."
Thou subtle God of Visions who hast led
My footsteps to this room, this hour, this night
That I might testify my resurrection.

Now song pours from a thousand instruments
And my new-opened eyes drink in the sound,
The seeing ear, the thinking, speaking heart,
Refreshed again after long banishments.

Praise for the dark that taught me love of light!
Praise for the ill that made me long for health,
Praise for the death that taught me all life is,
I praise the mortal wound that made me His!

The Anonymous

Swinging, hanging, on the windy hill
For nine long nights:
Lord of the Gallows, God of the sacrificed,
For whom no simple doom, no easier death sufficed,
But purchased with Your pain our happier plight.

Draw deep into Yourself the terrors of our life
Till, pierced by every wound
That man receives in his too vulnerable breast,
Poisoned spear, and sudden knife,
Reveal the life above, the deep death underground.

And in your last torment carry our final pain
Into the Valley of Joy; O in that last sigh,
Sad-drawn and patient, see the spell begins,
The blood stains dry, dispelled our sins
By that indrawn sigh.

The festivals begin on every street—
The scaffold falls in flame;
The guards depart, their swords are wreathed with
        flowers,
And long and slow their final footfalls beat.
Now we have purchased peace and fruitful hours.
But He? Where has He fled? What was His name?

The Visitation of Angels

When you entered the threshold with no pomp,
We saw the shadow of your aureole.
But its reflection lit the waiting room,
For a wonder's space, for a quick breath's flutter,
"Do you remember me?"

Beloved! Awaited! we have remembered you,
When you knelt in the bedchamber, when your shaking
    hand
Lifted the little child in its first blessing.
We saw you on the road when the first vision came,
And the disciples fled, and all the tormenters
Hissed at your name.
"Behold I shall send many messengers
In many forms and names."

And rising from our beds one winter night
We saw the city covered under grass,
Drowned under grass; trees bursting through the houses
And then the trumpets of Utopia
Disturbed the easy motion of our blood
And you were smiling softly through a cloud,
Uneasy, secret face.

Now is the time of revelation, visitation, now
Reveal yourself as when you walk through heaven,
The smiling soldier of the eternal wars,
And guardian of the Crown, the Sword, the Scepter,
The rose-shaped Jewel, and the Emerald Ring,
And the blue Brooch that bought the great betrayal,
The bleeding Ruby that can kill and heal,
And they all speak of you.

Slowly the lifestream learns its master-stream.
Slowly and murmuring in revolt we hear
Voices of love! (where no love was) sunlight, renewal
And for a moment feel the burning Jewel
Shining like blood against our mortal wound
By which our days are measured and subdued.
O then the vision breaks!
O then the Jewel speaks!

The Eyes

The children sing at night when they are frightened—
And I singing when my heart was heavy
Saw again the Eyes that filled the universe, that bright-
    ened
The withdrawn blood.
I saw them in the floating air when night unclasped its
    hood:
O but they are the same! eternally the same!
The long glance light-irised, the brilliant blue,
The middle vein of dark,
That sweet and powerful look,
And again the small house with deeper vision shook.

I too recall them. O my light, my joy, my hope, my
    woe!
Beautiful and unwelcome Eyes, that from falling steeps
    of sleep—
Fall, rise, and rising fall
(Cerulean, angelical);
Frequent your visitations now, I keep,
Remembrance of a face where you once lived,
Sensitive, glancing, gay,
Fixed forever on a blue flower that obscure, alone,
Illumined grass, softened stone;
The bright face and the blue flower vanished, but the
    Eyes stay—

Those Eyes in which I gazed my life away.

Vixen and Hound: The Lament of the Naiad

When streams ran dry and worshipers grew cold
And the green, speckled trout forsook my pool,
I rose to upper air, grew bold,
Felt earth its landscapes changing, manifold,
Skies dipped in rosy gray, the dappled clouds.

Still unaccustomed to the rooted ground—
With bruisèd feet, bright hair dishevelèd,
Ears ringing always with a fountain's sound,
The peopled world pursued me, vixen and hound;
I ran where peace is found.

Hollow and fierce the sunken eyes that peer
Protecting and unloving—
Zeal of Thy word O God, has pierced their ear,
Chaste, cold and just, Thy Name's fear,
Naked on naked stone.

Where is that bed of fern beneath the mountain
      peak?
Where drowned deep, deep, in love deep love con-
      ceived
The wild custodians of each brook and creek?
Their vigor runs from me, and far to seek
The tumult of their flying hair.

Law of the Unnamed God, dark, narrow, stern,
Thy love has dried my blood, Thy flame intense
Withers but cannot burn;
Thy glaring light pursues me when I turn
To fly my prison walls.

There stands the rock-sprung Church against the
      sky,

Dreading decay and bright unorthodox light,
Within the all-consuming, turning Eye;
Without the long-lost voices bid me fly
    I turn to fly, I stay, my skies, my streams, are
        gone!

The Innocent Rose

For a breath's space in the swan's summer
Of your unfolding years that like a deep rose opens,
Star-slow as a light in a dim ballroom
You move in running silver, drinking fluid music
From the great cup of crystal.
Spirit of the dance, a young girl in white muslin
And, breathing knowledge on the innocent breast,
The warm, conventional roses.

Step softly singing, from the swaying world
Before the cup of crystal breaks and shivers
Into the personal death.
The transient, fragile day filled full with overflowing
Delicately, O softly, cautiously,
Enter with music to your destiny
While your brief heaven is danced away.

Season of dawning life! spirit of the dancing foun-
    tain!
Spirit of the undying Rose! There with new eyes you
    sit—
The Rose itself. The soul of morning and of evening,
Iris and Hesper of the newborn world.

The Fête

Musicians, dancers, gather for the fête
On terraced lawns where marble cherubs wing
The unflying shafts.
And painted ladies linger late,
Their pastel satins faintly glimmering,
Light flowers on flowerlike breast,
Clipped from the garden's loveliest.

Moving like music to the flute's sound,
Masked girl and light beribboned courtier
Beneath the moon
Upon the moon-blanched ground—
Too trivial to be beautiful,
Yet the heart brims full

For an age's perfume strained, distilled, and
     pure
Till harsher airs disturb the century—
Thunder and long-pent rain
Strike the enchanted world grown insecure;
Nor does the dancing cease, nor do the dancers
     flee,
Still in a trance they move,
Without life, desire, or love.

Dancers and music fade in thinnest air,
Returning to the dying flowers their scent,
Their cut-flower elegance.
And what is left is neither sweet nor rare,
Trivial nor innocent;
The lightning shafts, the storm's rage
Scatters the sibyl's page.

The Golden Mirror

And you are startled when your reflected face
In the full midstream of your sight becomes
A mirror streaming back your secret light—
All private meaning brought to public day,
Your thoughts reflected in your eyes and brow;
Your fate runs in your blood.

The destined bloodstream purer, clearer, grown
And outward landscapes glow with inner gleams—
Now difficult roads grow smooth, familiar,
The invisible presence stalking all your ways
Becomes a living voice, an attractive face,
And the swift seasons all unnoticed run
While you count out your days.

As in your bewildered, hard and wistful Spring
The incredible hope was still to dream of Summer,
Or long for steel-fine cities gold with light—
Or brilliant windows glittering for your sake,
Or far green meadows known in reverie—

The meadows are your own, sometimes the windows
    shone
In that high city no man owns forever;
You stand in ripening fields, your task half-done,
The task half-done that is undone forever,
And know yourself a stranger in that meadow
Which now seems almost yours.

Begin to heed your pulsebeats, count the hours,
Or recognize your own face in the mirror,

The private meaning in the familiar glass.
Live deeply to your end while life pours in like sun,
As Rilke pricking his hand upon a rose
Signed joyously with his infected blood
The painful, personal death.

The Haunted House

The walls stripped of their pride remain the same,
Remain the same, though the great master's gift
No longer shines, reflects his glittering gift.
We change, we close the door and heart, we shift
Old acquisitions, older memories,
The treasures of the heretic moon and seas.

And now reflected on the luminous floor
The lamps send forth their golden melody.
The faded brocades of the sofas pour
The pressed-flower gentleness of mystery,
The longing that grows stronger and grows more.

Poor child who fades, too, by the aging door—
The chair from its fine curve of frailty
In wistful reverie caresses thee,
And the white ceilings of the evenings shake,
Traditional mildness against heartbreak.
Tomorrow and tomorrow wake and see
Your life speak in the forgotten tapestry.

These figures are your life, and these your soul
Out of which fruit and flowers roll and roll,
Through which the leaves of time forever fall—
Poor child who never feel their power at all,
So occult and subdued their spell,
So intricate the story they would tell.
The crystal chandeliers shed frozen tears
Of diamond light. The icy sockets burn.
Like newblown lilies in a Roman urn
Flushed with unborn sorrow,
The hour, the Presence, and the years,
Tomorrow and tomorrow and tomorrow . . .

The Castaways

No matter where they lived, the same dream came
Of the invisible landlady whose voice
Quickened the air with a dark flame;
The words they have always known, will always know
"You are unwanted! Go!"

And when they built a mansion and furnished it with art,
With love, with music, with the native flowers
It always happened, it was always the same:
The salon narrowed to a tomb,
Sometimes a servant's voice, or a voice from the chandelier,
"You have no business here."

And when they left for the remote island and became the idol
Of the indigenous tribe,
And were caressed, admired, and sheltered, then
Whose was the voice of blame?
That came when they assumed the garlands, the voice they knew
Saying, "This is not for you; this is all untrue."

And in the parks on Sundays with nursemaids, lovers, flowers,
And the bands playing and the fountains rising
In silver liquid hours,
Whose was the enemy? who was to blame?
If suddenly the observant shadows start
And cry, "Depart! depart!"

Now they have chosen exile, they have found a se-
    cluded house
In the smallest city, in the stillest shelter,
And they speak only to the wounded, the hunted, the lame,
The long evenings, the longer mornings, the longest noons;
And they wait for the bell to ring, for the landlady to appear;
And are they wanted here?

The Recall of Eurydice

Because the light still flowered in the heart
Where love and summer brimmed continually
The blue forest was hard to enter or depart
As the green mornings, and the living sea,
The embracing grass in which the cold snake slept.

But a firm black hand drew her gently down
Into that forest. Dim with the unpolished jewel
Of many a discarded life, each soul a forsaken town,
And in the obsequious dark her gentle eyes grew cruel,
And her forgotten hair fell shuddering down to her
  knees.

First like a maniac violin sounding among the tombs
Some lost voice descended, thrilled the dream-deep
  cypresses,
Swept through the trees, burst through the moving
  rooms,
Wild with the ancient sweetness of caresses
Remembered in the bitter strength of age,

Music that crept forbidden through the faint
Cerulean cypresses, the entangled drowning grass,
Raised in lament, in loss, in passion and complaint
Cleansing the mind, clearing the spirit's morass,
The remembered pain brought joy to the new dead.

The tie stronger than death, more exquisite than youth,
Than genius, beauty, grace, angelic sweetness,
Love has arrived himself divine among the uncouth,

The groping dead whose limbs have lost blood's fleet-
    ness
They behold One who conquers death with song.

To her the messenger came wing-sandaled, fire-
    aureoled
And dark buildings giddy with the sun
Opened their ancient windows, bell after bell tolled,
The long-locked river now began to run,
Only for her the new-lost, the recalled,

Her gray draperies shuddering in the wind
Lifted her ghostly wings. The compelling song, the
    wailing trees
Shook with supernal love for humankind.
"Farewell! Farewell!" she cried to shadows at her
    knees
Who wept remembering Time.

The music running through her awakened head
Recalled the bridal couch, the falling lakes, the
    streams,
The wistful daydreams of the maiden wed—
Or her love's form seen but through drowning gleams,
Through skyborn fragrance of the living flowers.

These she remembered when that backward look
Put out her eyes of vision and she fell
Into the firm black hands. Her fleshless body shook
In grief, and loss, and she returned to Hell,
Drank deep of Lethe and was still again,

A nameless shade, among the nameless shades.

Daydream and Testament of
Elizabeth Eleanor Siddall

Slowly my presence fades, glides from the room—
Nor shall you feel a deep particular void,
Nor shall I be a grim unconquerable specter
Rising among the forest trees at midnight,
Dreadful, compelling, a more terrible shape
Than seen by Dürer or Salvator Rosa,
To flit forever in a lurid gloom,
The spirit of the storm, and blasted tree.

But a quiet voice heard under glass or water
(Heard in a locked house behind crumbling walls),
The wide eyelids long as the slab of a tomb
Invoking the extreme, the Roman death
Of useless courage, and of needless patience:
"Courage! cold heart of stone."

Who heard the magnificent world's half-mocking
        laughter
And loved it most when it had most rejected;
Who born among the patient poor of cities
Saw with the frightened insight of the sick
The pale, the poverty-struck images
Lost between Limbo and eternity;

And felt with the keen anguish of the neglected
The dead walls, the iron railings—forever thwarted
Of life's full stream: kept always from the garden
By the hostile gardener, by the enemy footman.
Lying in the dark room on the uneasy bed,
I made a pavilion exquisite, distorted;
Heard bell-toned streams beating against stone walls,

Fire-aureoled angels, warm Venetian carnivals,
The daydream of the disinherited.

But there were faces grinning through the laurel
(Thin-drawn masks waxed white and always grinning),
Peering from stained-glass windows. What angel on
    the stair
Grew from ethereal beauty into nightmare?
The dark horizon narrowed, shrunken, closing
Until it crushed the heart, and the deep heavenly music
Floated unheard into a netherworld.
O what a chorus of hate! self-hate! world-wide betrayal
Pierced the closed heart, the sensitive, thin mind.

The drug by the bedside brought no further solace;
The gift of patience rotted into sloth,
Only the fantastic beauty woven into banners
Remains the triumph and the vindication.
The hallmark of the early dead, the ephemeral red,
The gold, the rose, of beauty now a legend
In the half-knowing half-believing hearts.
To be nothing, to know that Beauty alone is nothing,
Art itself is nothing, talent alone too common,
To have seen all come to nothing save despair,
Plumed like a silver dove: It carries a blazing poppy
From the indifferent or mocking skies.
Draw my bed upward to the skies! Or lower it under-
    ground!
And my hair will flame, will flower, in an imagined
    world
More real, more lovable, less strange than this.

The Affliction of William Cowper

> Nature revives again, but a soul once slain
> lives no more.
>
> —WILLIAM COWPER

The fear was always there. It lurked in early love;
It hid behind my mother's hidden eyes;
Riverfalls, mountains, glaciers of the soul
Rose upward in hysteria, and from pole to pole
I saw the morning fly. I saw the darkness rise,
And Satan descend in the form of a dove.

A soul once slain lives no more
But there were nymphs in the grotto, goldfish in the
     bowl,
The frivolous Duchess danced in the cotillion,
All powder, lace, and feathers; but I saw
The rent in the girdle, the beauty turned to baldness
And madness arrive a conqueror on a great stallion.

Hares in the garden, pigeons cooing tenderness,
But dead is the immortal soul that courted You,
Dreadful, implacable, God, Judge, Lover, Tormentor.
We are the marked of Heaven who dare not speak
The singled-for-damnation, the unique—
The vain, sad hours descend, from skies of gentler
     blue.

Soft skies of shifting azure drowned in delicate light,
I saw Your blazing Center thick with night,
I hear my doom announced in a quiet voice
And know of no appeal. There is no hope, no choice.
I retire to the small house in a village street,

Hear from the harpsichord a tinkling sharp, clear,
    sweet.

Or a woman's voice in tender pathos singing,
A rabbit's furtive run outdoors, a silken garment's
    flounce,
Or, best of all, see grass in freshness springing
Out of the kindly earth, the warm maternal breast
(Our perilous Mother at her loveliest),
And hear the Father's voice demand, command, de-
    nounce.

Secure, innocent, peaceful, but the thistle sorrow
Will rise some unexpected day in some idyllic hour;
It will speak through a bird, it will breathe through
    a flower;
The feared, enchanting face may come in sleep
And draw me through blue forests twisted, tangled,
    deep
Into some vast obsession called *"Tomorrow."*

And Ann may sing, and Mary play, and the fire burn
And frost and wind outside make shelter sweet—
But a gulf opens and I try to name the sin
That drew me slowly to the steep ravine,
That flung me into the abyss; I strive to name the turn,
The subtle flaw, that made destruction fleet.

Solitary, cut off from hope, the stricken deer
Pierced by the wrath of God—it faints in solitude,
Sees luster of the Heavens washed and clear,
Made sacred by young light, made human by a tear,
The human tear that reaches Heaven's Lord
And is as poignant as a prayer, as wounding as a
    sword.

In that vast gulf between my God and me
No prayer can fly, no sword can pierce the heart

That is cast out by Him, and sinks alone apart.
Some invisible guard pushes the poison from our
     hand,
The knife pressed to the heart breaks—
A warning bell its iron music shakes.

The rope falls from the gibbet, and condemned to
     breath,
An agony of steep eternity;
Forever in the interior dark, I sit and write;
While the black Presence shades the simple land,
Tranquil I sit. I write the beautiful clear prose
From which my sorrow rises like a rose,
Floats through the garden and the lonely heath

Till all my agony is purged of endless night
Into that downfalling stream, a drowning laurel
     wreath.

The Madness of Jean Jacques Rousseau

Aging, forsaken, passionate, and unloved,
Neighbors stone me. Silence blackens my door,
Knives always at my breast, but at my century's throat
I, too, can press a knife, inflict the healing wound;
I see the classic statues dripping blood.

As I appear, the harassed, murdered man,
Father of the castaways, lover of the damned,
The conqueror of the Alpine solitudes,
The walker on the abyss, the swan's interpreter,
When her dissolving image stains the world.

The east trumpet signals. On the lake
The brilliant glaciers melt! The orphaned children
    beckon,
All whom the earth disowns and God forgets
(And in the gilded salons tears are falling).
I appear. I speak. I hold a book in my hand.

The Tempest

As in a Watteau fête of rose and silver blue
The intense colors lift the dreamy world
Into a sharper vision than it knew,
The graceful figures vast in miniature

And deepens overhead the delicate, sweeping azure—

So in the cold and limpid morning air,
When but a hint of sun was felt, we breathed the storm,
Companioned by young light. It touched the warm,
Half-sleeping flowers. Unseen, but everywhere
We felt the tempest's uncreated form

Gathering its might, its bright and nervous flare.

See how its silver hand unveils the clouds!
And the soul's solitude in anger wakes
The waving reverie of grass, and whispering shakes
The airy heavens into the drifting lakes

While rain falls gently from the savage eyes,

And silken-sharp the dazzling thunder falls
Upon the startled land: The rising, falling dart
Sudden and piercing in the summer's heart.
And while from tree to tree the voice of fire calls,

The unleashed tempest shakes the garden walls.

The Rose, the Fountain, the Mirror

See how my fountain in autumnal air
Sheds frozen water on the changing garden—
Time's bright betrayal all unnoticed there:
Sweet promises of summer, spring's vivacious season
When the fresh waters danced towards leaves of May,
And joy and hope gleamed gay beyond all treason
And all was tender light and fulfilled day.

Now let the icy water be a glass
In which the one thought like a rose must fall
(A broken rose that once seemed large, too large,
In some distorted, half-remembered carnival
Or flaming image seen in a mirage):
On you will my eyes rest, my mind repose—
O fountained mirror where the self must float
Lost and forgotten as the drowning rose.

The Angel of the Solitary

Always from brilliant windows peering
The unknown woman's striking face,
All dark and white and shadow-lit—
I see her wayward figure flit,
Forever here, then disappearing,
Her blue-gray gown, clouds of lace,
Her plumed black hat, her gloves of gray,
The spirit of that secluded place:
A great and weatherworn hotel
Perched on a lake of birch and fir.

And floating eyes will follow her
From echoing corridor, suite, salon,
Or heavy, shaded dining hall
Where whispers echo, die, and fall.
Indifferent, familiar,
She walks where furtive figures stir
Each solitary reveler,
Always tranquil and alone,
Where men in final stupor sit
And the last, dwindling lights are lit.

Among tobacco fumes, the wine,
I see her pure, pale aura shine,
I see her earrings' deepest jet,
See on her moving bosom glow
The antique old gold cameo.
Wherever her light footsteps press—
Falling, flowing, from her dress
The scent of Parma's violet.

She hears as if from Limbo sent
A fiddle raised in harsh lament
Following her footsteps. Piercing, sweet,

A song as sharp as death, or sin,
Sweeps upward from the violin,
Floats overhead and under feet.

Mysterious spirit of the wine,
Grave and reserved and punctual,
You pass between the drunken scene
Casting a shadow on the wall.
Where the gross fails in the divine,
The sacred blends in the obscene,
Unheeding of dark winds that call,
You move, where Time's inverted torch
Shines like a thin spire on a church.

I watch and watching, trembling, know
That you will come, that you will go
From dull-draped rooms of horror sent
To be each man's presentiment.
There where the wines of Lethe flow
(As cool as water, bright as snow)
Neither on good nor evil bent,
Your image to each wine glass sent
Obscures the grief that all would bury,
The angel of the solitary!

The Nativity

Through the pure air of mountains your first breath
Drew in ancestral charm, a love of heights and clarity,
Desire in a small room defying death—
Opened the enchanting eyelids, warmed the blood
Into a beauty passionate and meek.

What, O thou gentle spirit newly born,
Did you ask from the cold air? what did you seek?
He answered "Life!" To move with the stormy cloud,
To hear the trapped, lost hunter's silenced horn,
To embrace destiny in her glittering shroud.

The Silent Day

So rings the silence, so the high days pass
Without sound or motion on the land:
Immovable, intact, the seasons stand
Like mirrored images in polished glass.

When will a voice destroy this silence, break
The chill of autumn in my summer sky?
If but a flower blown by the wind would sigh
And shatter quiet for a memory's sake,

If but a leaf would fall, if but a wing would stir,
From some fantastic heaven my blood would leap,
The burden lighten and grow easier—
This solitude is sleep, falls steep, grows deep.

The Companion

Only when the golden light forsakes the meadow
In the exhausted twilight, in the lonely evening,
Do you see the dark-eyed, white-winged shadow
Moving like autumn mist among the yellow daisies?

Among the yellow daisies, the burning sun-struck grass,
Like leaves on air the small feet soft descending,
Moving like sudden love, certain as destiny,
Light as the touch of hope, as keen as sorrow.

She moves to your hidden heart, she lingers there,
Fills the tight-sealed room with secret glory,
Dances through your eyes, breathes through your hair,
Flickering like sun between the fall and summer.

Tender the childish hand on the tired, stooped shoulder,
Soft is her smile upon the sullen eyes,
Where her voice leads the answering quiet remembers,
She unlocks my eyes, the withdrawn heart grows bolder.

Quiet playmate, always near, the dream's companion,
Flesh of my spirit, slight and childish angel
Sprung from the body's pain, glowing through fire's failure,
I had expected some divine, some greater thing—

Some Goddess, Juno-browed, bearing the sign of the Father,
Some seaborn Loveliness flushed with the rose of dawn,
Some Messenger from Heaven, sky-eyed, star-gleaming,
Some beautiful Archer armed with the flying death.

But in a small room, in the ripened air of summer
My destiny approaches smaller than I have dreamed—

A growing girl, star-shod, who swiftly enters:
In her thin hands she holds a glittering missal.

Together we decipher the crimson-lettered volume,
She leaning over my shoulder speaks the benediction,
In her young voice as clear and pure as a pearl;
And through the assenting quiet, a far-off clavier answers.

"All Is Well with the Child"

I saw you arise from your bed, I saw your door open
Into a room flowering and falling with flame,

Into that room you came.

I feared for you, I followed, I called your name:

And you walked unharmed through the fire three times in
    flame,
You plunged and scorched to the soul returned, renewed,
    unharmed,
And the flames thinned to ashes, fell in a waiting urn.

Pallid with dying light I saw the day return.

No mind could penetrate, no eye discern
In what perpetual lives and deaths you breathed and drew
Strength for another life, another death.
That all was well with you the awakening sunlight knew.

Then without anguish, indifferent, calm, and reconciled
I heard the voice of my heart: "All is well with the child,"
And lilacs sprang into bloom, it was spring, the air was mild,

And again the voice said: "All is well with the child."

FROM *Selected Poems*

1954

Lady Asleep upon a Leaf

(After a Chinese Painting)

Lightest of aerial things, a flower, a feather
Is no lighter than you who sway
On an invisible bough
Through jasmine-scented air
In the May weather . . .

Veiled in a golden haze
(Frail, short-lived like the flowers),
Above you, and before
The pensive drooping hours
Expand in cycles, grow
Under the invisible bough
In the May-mild air . . .

The long hours gliding glow
In a white and silver gleam,
Faint in the white cold
And sun-gold streams of your hair,
Sleep now
Under the invisible bough
In the flower-haunted air . . .

The Wedding Ring

(Mrs. William Morris)

The moments in a garden, or the air
That blew one summer and swept your youth away,
The swish of your silk skirt, or the light touch
(Light and yet overmuch)
That left its deepest imprint on the dark.
Old house! dead world! worn dream! that sways and
　　falls,
Lulled heartbeats, dulled footfalls
All in oblivion's transcript recorded
Implores eternal quiet, yet recalls
The smoldering beauty of the fiery head,
Tales of the flowering branches stripped and bare
Within a dulled gold sphere.

Never your image clear
Or opening of a heart that may have broke
But never spoke.
Among the cypresses and orange trees
Where as moon-goddess, or Proserpine,
You moved among strange forms, or mysteries,
Or that La Pia, traveler Dante saw
(Waylaying him at Purgatory's door),
Whom legend clothes with a mysterious death—
So you encounter me
And veil and half unclothe your mystery.

"Remember me who was La Pia. Me
Whom first Siena made, Maremma then unmade,
O love, O withering,
O fires that brushed my bridal hem

Woven in rosy coronal, or gold diadem!
Love that survives within one rounded sphere
Withholds its ambiguities
And one who can will not break silences
Round year on rolling year
He who in plighting troth, first wed me with his
      ring."

The Entrance to Saint Sophia's

Swiftly as country dogs through deepwoods leaping,
Through falling, flashing waterfalls, through high,
    through wide,
Rousing warm summer from her golden sleeping,
Here, here, the gay athletic heroes come—
Like exiled emperors from Byzantium
Unblinded they await
The entrance to Sophia's glittering gate.

Irene, or Eudoxia,
Justinian, Belisarius,
Comneni, Palaeologus,
Cyril, John of the Golden Mouth,
Saints, emperors, or warriors,
The purple-clothed, the terror-crowned, they come,
Through the silenced circuses, the conquered city
Where the gilt cross has fallen, and lies lost
Under the blood and guilt of centuries

That blood and guilt reveal, and God is seen
Walking blue waves—green, green
Is the holy city of Constantine.

Louder, louder, the drum
Where exiled heroes come.
Who shall restore their visionary home?
Now that the cold winds rage,
Now that their leaf-light spirits burn,
They claim their heritage;
Mosaic, ikon flame,
On their half-buried name
When, when, will they return?

The far-off splendor of Sophia's dome,
Not History but the Spirit's city,
Glittering, golden, glorious,

Floating above the sacred Bosporus.

The Initiation
(After Baron Friedrich von Hügel)

I saw the Savior's suffering drowned in joy,
That sorrow sky-deep as eternity
Flowed inward through the soul's deep privacy;

I saw how faith had colored the deep rose,
Transfigured suffering into suffused glory:
In His love is our repose,
In His death our fount of joy,
In His anonymous pang our story.

In the Borghese gardens thick with summer
There once von Hügel sat, an aging, sick newcomer—
Heavy with sorrow, failure, pettiness,
Antipathies, grievances, all hope undone
With useless striving toward each crumbling year:

And saw through living Rome, Rome's stony centuries
Revolve in beauty through the golden trees;
The aerial hand of time raised to arrest and freeze
The patient generations on their knees—
Pagans and saints bright in oblivion,
All marked by suffering, or consumed by sin

Beneath the lucid sun; the dark-rimmed mystery,
The hostile road that leads to sanctity,
Quo Vadis Master? and I felt soft, deep and still
Within the gardens His pervading will.
Our lives are but His thought, and if we wish, we see
Beneath the Mystery the unfolding sea.

Flight of the Sparrows

Sparrows through the winters flying
Over misted roof and sky,
Clinging to the wind and sighing
In a gray immensity,

The immense sky and towers,
While below the small, brown lives
Crawl in time, the whirling hours
Burned away in narrow hives.

Then the soul in indignation
Tore its frantic way in flight
To fantastic contemplation
Of the splendors of the night;

Dreamed of peacocks, glittering, gold,
Trees whose happy branches spread
Into landscapes free and bold—
Expanding daystreams overhead.

Slowly, slowly, year by year,
In an angry flight defying,
You escape—return to clear
Cold winters where the sparrows veer,

Through the desperate city flying.

May Morning: Hudson Pastoral

The morning of the world, the western afternoon,
Cold on the American green, eternal youth renewing
Even as on Hudson's stream—
Cole, Inness, Durand, fixed the legend and gleam,

Made mythical that beauty, freshness, wildness
Pierced by a light, thin-bright as gold-spun hair;
The genius of the place in ecstasy
Rose naked in a young antiquity.

And saw with eyes pure-chill as the May breeze,
The young America that ripened there—
Classic and Gothic shadows interlaced,
Green-dappled, dancing streams embraced.

Dear, sky-rapt stream, O green-reflecting river,
Wait, wait, for one whose music long delayed
Your foam-green branches seek—
Seek, find their flowering tongues and speak,

Speak in the white lilac's breath, the narcissi's spear,
Purple-fanged iris, pink-flushed apple spray,
Each flower-frail world that flows
To reach the season of the rose.

Upon the white veranda one will stand
Until light's revelation grows so fine
It seems time's silver-silenced shoes
Are worn by Bryant's or by Freneau's muse

And the evasive river silver-silent, gliding,
Gathers its green-garnered, legend-growing treasury,
Opens its watery arms and singing, sliding; runs
To deeper gold, and copper-coinèd suns.

Nocturnal

And now no more. The evening song is over.
The silver night with its clear shining eyes
Of starry light descends; the moon's flambeau
Floods widening terraces in deepening glow
And the lake waters sing as to a lover.

Pierced by the keen, articulate surprise
We'll go no more where tranquil waters flow,
Or where the moonstruck hills drink burning snow,
Or where, long-stemmed and lonely, white and cool,
The water lilies tremble on the pool.

Night Music

I have learned to like dying trees and black meadows;
Swamps have their grace and fogs their sweetness;
Even the cold that locks the winter door
Strengthens, sustains the higher, dryer spirit.

How clear all things! the seasonal fires leap
Still unexhausted through the darkening windows.
I see again life's legendary face,
The shuttered brilliance of her eyes grown wide
And the wild hair now smoothly shades her brow.

Leaves, days, hopes, friends fall surely, cruelly now;
Snow and the rain greet you. Loved voices now half-
    silent
Sing imperceptibly their muted music.

The Twisted Tree

Too brief the sunlight when it smote
Our summer-haunted life! but caught
The dark tree's slowly brightening thought,
Saw fruit of fire and snow
Upon the topmost bough
And felt with love that gaze of fire—
The body sick with lost desire—
And heard the sad, once lovely note
Through choirs of change and evening float
Beneath the twisted tree,
The twisted spellbound tree.

I heard the bird of morning sing,
Rise phoenix-like and shimmering
In sudden holiday.
We let our forgotten bodies air
In streams of daybreak freshening, new,
And saw the sky's recurrent blue
Through dark and cold, through fire and dew:
The bird sang everywhere
Beneath the trembling tree,
The shivering storm-wracked tree.

Then in our bones and in our blood
The black autumnal flood
Ran clear in sleeping veins and ran
Through pure wild sunburst, and the air
Revealed its sun-struck beauty—joy!
Joy! Joy reborn leaped into flower!
Once more Joy blessed the living hour,
Lit up the twisted tree,
The nine-time twisted tree of death.

The Negress in the Coach

The Negress' head peering out of the old coach,
Floating across some mushroom-scented road,
A Lithuanian castle standing high;
It has seen the Tartar horseman flying by
And heard the sudden shriek, the startled cry,
Known arrow, javelin, the point of the sword
And the iron clamor of the Golden Horde.

Why do my unwilling, sullen dreams present
Images from some reluctant memory?
Those forms, slant-eyed, fur-capped, magnificent,
Riding forever through the castle gate,
Faster and faster, dim as mortal fate.

Why in the emblazoned coach the Negress peering
        through,
An alien to that snowbound, pain-drenched earth
(And windows glimmering in that northern blue),
She in a blazing world foresaw a warmer dearth?
And yet reveals those racial dreams where I
Can never find a home or place to die?

For in my dreams the horsemen always fly
(Barren their conquest, lost their victory)
While backward out of space the old coach lumbering
        keels
And the spent wave of Time recoils and reels.

Recall the Mongol prince or bid the carriage halt,
Follow the Negress where she moves in state,
Stand at the castle door with bread and salt
And offer to the enthroned, the conquering chief
The homage traditional, eloquent and brief.

And hear, while summers burn and winters freeze
And winds scythe through the autumn leaf by leaf,
Stamping of horses, and the ancient dead,
The Power that guides the disinherited,
The dark faces and the slow approach,
The rumbling, occupied, emblazoned coach,
Its nameless mystery and ancient dread.

The Mirrored Room

Into the mirrored room, her eyes glazed and remote,
She walked silk-shod upon gold,
Winter silver, the summer gold,
Death shivered in her fur coat.

All things she touched grew clean and clear,
The china clock, the gilded chair
Assumed a rigid, classic air;
The golden haze grew high, austere.

The curtains hung mute, motionless;
Through noontide windows the sun dial
Brimmed thick with dark. A little while
All things seemed dim but her red silk streaming
    dress.

Through doors of glass and chill we heard
That dreamy, gentle, and unhuman
Voice that was not of mortal woman
Nor voice of angel, nor of bird.

We followed her through waves of frost
And saw her multiple figures pass
Floating through walls of ice and glass,
The guardians of the trapped, tamed, lost.

"Why, why, chill lady, fur-wrapped, virgin cold,
Does your red gown shed color and flame
Upon a fear that has no name,
Why turn to silver all our gold?

And why the silent sidelong look,
The glance that burns the world away,
Cold as the streams of a mountain brook
Yet vivid as the eye of day?"

The Sleeper

On tiptoe to the forgotten land
Where memory plunges, steep and wide,
Through uplands stretching toward the sea
And silver-sliding river-side,
Led by the season's glowing hand
I found the sleeping Love,
Naked in a green grove.

Rose petals rained upon his head;
Slumber-soft a velvet shower,
Light, bright, and fragrant seemed to stir
Each fallen noontide hour
That shone in sunstreams overhead
Till the locked eyes of sleep
Opened on ever-deepening deep.

There did he lie, and there we stood,
Who watched the naked boy,
Unarmed, defenseless, sleep away
The warm blood's living flood,
And the cold streams of joy
The lifelong summer day.

Heart, heart, when he awakes, the rain
Will surely fall, the storms will blow
And all the rose-trees stir in vain
To arrest their savage overthrow;
Uneasy shapes and presences
Shiver and speak—and then abstain,

Tower in emptiness—and growing tall
Will overshadow all.

And no escape, I see Love wake
And shake bright danger from his eyes,
Mysterious as the midnight lake
That wakes to fresher dawns than ours.
Now cloud horizons clear and rise,
Fierce as the Caribbean showers
Whose lyric violence overpowers
The eager life that longs to leap
Out of its golden sleep.

A Friend's Song

Soon to reach you where you are—
Far away—O dear to me,
Far away and very far
From silence and hostility
Rise the cities where you roam
Far away and far from home.

Stretching out my spirit hand,
I can touch you where you lie
In the much-contested land
Where the wounded heroes sigh,
Far away the lullaby
Of the sullen beach and strand,
Far away and far from me.

Neither rock, nor reef, nor snow,
Neither death nor calumny,
Neither the wild stress and flow
Of storm and tempest, wind and woe
Of the shipwreck-ridden sea
Can turn, or change, or take from me
Longing, love, and constancy.

Song of the Girl in the Red Cloak

"Are flowers the winter's choice,
Is Love's bed always snow?"
I heard that far-off voice
Cry, "No!" cry, "No!"
But the door was locked
And the voice mocked.

Snow was your summer bed,
The flowers bowed down and died
And all the books you read
And all the voices lied
Save one Book alone
Written in flame on stone.

Flowers, snow, ice, snow, fire
Crowded into one hour;
There she sat behind barbed wire;
A relentless shower
Beat against her window-pane
Ice, rain, sleet, rain:

The girl in her cloak of flame,
Drawn was her face; and slow
Her long hours drift and flow—
She has forgotten her name,
And the far-off voice:
"Is Love's bed always snow?
Are flowers the winter's choice?"

Song of the Forsaken Lilac Tree

Year after year the moon
Struck the illimitable silences and now
It glitters on the snow;
Soon it will freeze the little lilac tree
That longs to bloom and grow.

The fresh season tuned its leaves,
Heart-shaped, purple-laden,
Where now the immense silence grieves.
Some lonely maiden
Gathers the unseen sheaves,

The graceful blossoms and their piercing scent,
The beauty burning fine and innocent,
Fainting beneath the moon
And the air trembles and the solitude
Sinks in this lunar swoon.

I shall not see my lilacs clear the air
In bursting fountains of spring's essence glowing
Upon the deserted stair
In that neglected house and garden where
Memory retains its fixed and guilty stare.

Flower and tree and scent through time sway.
The moon will carry the guilt away—
It was not meant to stay.

The Intruder

Have you no eyes for me?
Whose wings have often beat
Against your window-seat
Dear love, let, let me in.

So wasted white, and thin
And dulling piteously
From long trial and denial,
Dear love, let, let me in.

"The hour is late, the night
Ingrown within my breast,
Too late for all delight
And sleep is best."

No, loosen your dark hair
And gaze long, deep, and still;
You cannot fly nor kill
The winged immortal joy,
The flowering love.

Offering and Dedication

Ladies of Helicon, these dew-damp roses
Accept as offering to your glass-cool fountain
With its miraculous sprays of ice-clear water
Leaping into the shimmering summer sky.

Maidens who guard the immortal source of song,
My days, hours, years, in fiery cold consumed
Plunge through wild fancy in your tranquil stream,
Through instinct learn your rock-rough, island sea-
    scape.

Where the wild rose springs from the split rock
I knelt; and plucking bloom from the living stone
I fill my arms and make the ancient tribute
To the unfailing fount of Helicon.

Where sun-bright trees bend low in brimming water
Wild thyme, dark laurel drooping low I offer

This rose, this dark damp laurel, this green thyme.

FROM *Terraces of Light*

1960

The poems from the Italian of Michelangelo Buonarroti (page 194) and of Lorenzo de' Medici (page 195) are hitherto unpublished; they are placed in this section, with the other translations from *Terraces of Light*, for reasons of continuity.

Time and Atlantis

Above the hanging gardens she looked down
While the dark river flowed beneath the tower.
There, there was calm; there, there fertility;
On the stone terrace blazed the fiery flower;
Unknown, untamed the black Euphrates rolled;
The centuries were drowned and spoke no more.

Over the balustrade the queen's hair flowed
But golden summer in her southern lair
Walked like a lion among the yellow roses,
Glittered like gold thread in the queen's gown,
While from the hanging gardens she looked down

On pinnacles, gardens, sculptured beasts, hot stone
Between the hanging gardens and the heavens.
Outside the desert stretched; the unshaded land
Burned in the long monotony of heat,
While, from the hanging gardens, she looked down.

Languid and heavy for a summer's span,
Between the rose-world and the barbarian
Whose desert shadow mocks the flowering world,
Withers the garden, shakes the rose leaf down,
Darkens the drooping eyelids of the queen:
Only the desert shines—a painted scene.

But wait! This hour is light, the terrace shines;
The melting sun beats on the orange tree,
The sun-drenched palm, the scented, slipping vine—
Falls in an azure-veiled serenity:
The crouching lions, through tropic sunshafts shown.

While from the hanging gardens she looked down,
The great queen's eyelids woo the ungentle skies,

Remembers some cold fountain's limpid noise,
Remembers lost Atlantis' brilliant isles
Drowned in the dark floods of eternity,
In a wild sweep, through a great sea hurled
Between the rising and the drowning world.

Variation on a Polish Folk Song

Joy! Joy! Joy! that on my quiet day
In the dull house where never a sound
Echoed and entered, where I sat forever waiting,
The long, gray shadow crossed my way;
I saw the renowned greyhound
Speeding across dry fields, across my floor,
So clean, sand-sprinkled, poor.

An ardent beast, half-tamed, hesitating,
I thought him till his eyes shot flame;
They seemed to call me to the illimitable lands
Into the very far,
Till I forgot my world, my life, my name.
And then I heard the unearthly wail of a horn
Sound from the world of the unborn.
And a red-ringed falling star—
And galloping across my field on a black horse,
A lone, fiery Hussar,
Who smiled and looked at me
While the great greyhound licked my hands.

Gently he waits, his mute eyes speak to me
(Unintelligible and irresistible the call!)
Of the great, patient animal
Who spoke in the Hussar's eyes,
Who drove his madman's course,
Flies skyward with my soul on his black horse
Toward some great, groaning sea,
Who sends his greyhound emissary!

Day after day I lie and talk to him,
Helpless on my sick-bed,
In the mute language of the seraphim;

And by unbearable longing led,
My closing eyes are humbly questioning.
Tell me, O lean, fierce creature, gently bred,
Of your Master, the Lord of the Dead,
Who brings such learning to the poor unread,
Whom the falling constellations bring,
And the tempest's whirling wing,
Who takes the Hussar's form,
And rides in angry beauty through the storm!

The Fountains of Rome

I

Look at Bernini's angels as they rise
To the sunrise of trumpets and the bounds
Of the skies' vaulted and imperial eyes,
The cries of cherubim who lift their marble covers
From the long dark—
From quilts of lapis-lazuli they rise, from a bed
Of tasseled gold and red
They leave the uplifted fountains blessed by God,
Celestial sights and sounds—
Read through the cracks and stains
The crumbling signatures of time and tombs,
The heraldic and majestic glooms
Of leaping fountains bursting through the day
In lives of foam and spray.
Constant, cool, are they;
They fly the confining world's imprisoned room,
They lift the cross above the pagan waters,
Relieve the ancient watch of Neptune's green-haired
    daughters.
Refreshed, they feel again
The *vivat* and the rushing of the rain
On the dry spirit and the sunburnt plain.

II

Flights and finesse of waters, from what rock
Or time-drowned aqueduct or living springs you come?
(The wheels of resurrection turn and hum)
The mind's long apathy to living sources turn
The fountains leap again in diamond glow and shock.
O Rome, your steady Rock
Retains an older glow,

Now, even, now,
Through quickening rain, through rainbow stream;
It stands while tempests mock.
Through heat, through cold, through rose, through
    snow
With carved uplifted hair as in a dream
Bernini's angels fly and gleam.

III

Flow, flow, dark years and at the Fountainhead
The world behind the visible world is shed
And glows in clearest silver, runs in thickest gold,
In aerial draperies, in sea-whorl fold.

Slow, liquid years, flow to that Fountainhead
Where all our days lie down on that vast bed,
Are plunged in depths, are lost, or harvested
Are scattered, rifled, planted, murdered or wed.

The Waiting

I

Uplifted birds who into burning skies
Soar deep and wait:
I see but this quiet house, this frozen road,
Feel it expand, dilate—
But know a glooming tiger at my gate
Unseen by other eyes.

Tell me, dark daughters of Jerusalem
Who saw the Sacred Word
Take wing transformed to a bird,
You saw it wound the sky
And burn the sun away
And hover through the silence where I stray—

Have you not seen another watching one
Who blasts the morning, shades the evening sun,
Toward whom all streams of silence run
In singing unison,
For whom the small birds fly
Wild-piercing and elate,
Who shields the sleeping tiger at my gate
And mocks me while I wait?

II

Sunlights of youth, cascades, springs, waterfalls,
Cold fountains of desire, plunge, plunge, aspire
To reach that heart of fire
That glows with dark, with light—
That Sun of life that moves, that still recalls
The changing world's delight,

Rose-dipped and golden flame.
O love above all loves it is your name
That circles round the heavens where you yearn
And will someday return.

III

You of the delicate eyelids and soft speech
My golden daughter walking on the strand
Of an old alien land
Among bright streams and cascades, veiled in light.
I see you turn your garden gate
And sun streams from your aerial form; you turn
To where the wild birds yearn,
Your heartbeats are the universe, you reach
The silver fountains of the night
Alone and not afraid—
You see the lilies of the winter fade
In shade, in softest shade.

The Flowing of the River

Without remorse, without regret, without fear, without envy
I watch the flowing of the river as flows my life away.

Unperturbed by the bold wind rising and the surf beating
On the storm-cleansed coast, refreshing the northern sky

With wind and waves and waters, with wild motion and joy
Never still, never fearful, happy in deep dark plunging—

Beautiful the mornings, unveiled by the Dawn's white hand
Striking out time from the crystal clock of the hours.

The icebound streams now clear, forever released from winter,
Melt in the sun and shine, in a shower of stars and spray,

Tranquil and cool, active, wavering, winding, unweaving flow
Bright waves! dripping in sun, as a seabird unruffles its wings.

Whose are the drowning eyes plunged deep in deeper, deeper
    depth
Rising in circling gleams of light, mournful at nightfall?

Foretelling the season of silence, dreaming always of summer
Southward and ever southward, the wavering, windworn
    waters flow.

Cloud Carnivals

Child, you have played too long;
Why will you seek the sky?
Earth was so pleasant once,
Its colors soothed the eye:
Wide, wide, its boundaries
And its never weary seas.
The heart and the brain
So pleasantly content,
There all things seem to please.
It is late, it is cold—
O heavenly banishment.

But I have grown to love
These floating lakes of air
And the gray shifting rose
Of the cloudy forests
Islands and airy seas
Moving in dove-gray flame
Silver-blue edged with fire
And then the clouds! the clouds!
That sail and swim above
The ever moving skies
When dark-browed Evening lies
Deep, dark with starlit eyes,
Deep, dark, with many eyes.

Elegy and Nocturne for Lora Baxter

Within the waxen lotus gleams the jewel.
Stretch out your hand, lost friend, and touch it where
Illumination shadows your white hand, bright hair
That like water in a pale stream
Flows where the brilliant ice-peaks burn and gleam.

This was your sun-filled life; it leaped, it glowed,
A jewel in the lotus heart, light fell in diamond clusters,
The mountain peaks loomed high, bright passions fever-high
Poured a white light at noon like the moon's silver, thrown
On a blue river's ever-changing lusters.

Lovely were the hours—
Happy, happy were the birds that sang above the short-lived
        flowers,
Green-breasted, scarlet-winged, and emerald, tawny, dap-
        pled,
Never again such color, such music, happy, upspringing
        free.
Do they sing still in your vast sea?

Nocturne

Gold showered into the water, sunset drowns
The completed freshness of the waking day;
But when the darkness veils the trees and when
The heightened pulses of the world beat low,
Only the golden light in afterglow
Prepares us for the closing of the way—
Nightfall before we know—she of the shadowed hair
Blue-tinted as the sky, unbound and undulating
As the silver-streaming river; it is she,
The nymph of unquiet and despair, whom night and
    the river bring,
Sorrow from silence rising frantically,
Nymph of the dark night whose despair and rage
Only the moon-gold and night-cold assuage.

Terraces of Light

Where the drowsy landscape draws
Summer from a floating Eye;
Where the winding pathways lie
Expanding in gold rings of light,
Quivering, falling bright on bright;
Where the cup of dew is spent
In the glittering light of day,
Let us mount the steep ascent
To the castle, see the way!
Where the sleep-worn bastion towers,
Shimmering in a falling haze,
Hanging mountains, twisted trees
Chill the running golden spray.

That ascent will bring us near
To the castle in the sky
Where the cloud foundations rise
On the brilliant atmosphere.
Further, further lies the prize
That man seeks before he dies
(Where the impelling hunger leads);
The visionary landscape pleads,
The more than life-size roses sigh—
You have left the world behind,
Chilled the heart and drugged the mind
Seeking what you cannot find.

In the shadow of that Eye
Floating in an azure stream,
We have mounted dream on dream
To the terraces of light,
Shed our lives away like leaves
That the first faint chill bereaves
Of volition—and lets fall

The season's measured festival,
Dropping in cold pools of thought,
All we treasured, all we sought,
And slowly, slowly, withering
The maimed, unfeeling, senses sting.

But through hanging waterfalls
Striking against greenest green,
Hardly hoping, scarcely seen
We have reached the castle walls
Entered through the mildewed halls
Seen the prostrate shadows flee
Forms of fear and fantasy
Cloaked in everlasting night,
Fleeing in a blaze of light.

Time and the Mower

FOR PATRICK

The bright world dims, the sea
Of time rolls hastily
And overfloods the bank.
Shaded the summer roses;
Where did the lilacs go
Into what waste of snow?

After the heat the calm,
After the pine, the palm,
Eternity appraises
The long years that are gone
And her long upward look
Smiles on the fading book.

There is a center of joy
No turn of tides destroy:
That kindness flowing ever,
That beauty and that bounty
Without reserve or end.
There is that long-sought friend
Who will desert you never,
Returning in His Name
To the great central flame.

Doubtful, the rough sea tide
Beats on the cold hillside,
Restrains the unruly passion
Distorts, derides and chills
Even when need be kills—

Yet knows a Presence stands
In the unchanging lands.

With a glance of fire, with a look
Of power the fort was taken;
The defenses are all down,
Sacked, razed, the stubborn town,
The rivers are all flooded:
Where are those endless vistas?
With a sharp sickle the mowers
Cut and cannot destroy
The ever springing joy,
The bright immortal hours
Plucked by the fatal sisters.

Deep Dark with Many Eyes

He has many eyes that pierce without, within.
Nothing can hide from him, even the dead
Though buried deep will rise invisibly
When he can penetrate their dark; they feel, they see
He is the Master of all mystery
Whom the floods and tides obey.

Turning and burning the worn years away,
A force none can gainsay,
He seeks through darkness, finds the trembling day,
Bids her come forth
From the soul's frozen north—
Springing and spreading in a wild excess
Of all consuming blessedness.
Yet I have seen him like a falling star
Dissolve into a flower of light
When his all-seeing glance puts out my sight!

The Release of Ariel

The unravished soul slips free, unbound
The silver chains, the cloven pine
Unmemoried falls, and Time unwound
Burst into bright
Cycles of incandescent light.

The recovered earth drinks up the dew,
The free grass waving masterless
Lies light beneath blue worlds I knew:
Ariel and Caliban,
Angel and beast, one man.

Free in a world once mine, not mine,
I hear the Master's farewell saying
(Smiling), "Quick spirit, earth is thine,
Stars, trees, skies, birds—
The music innocent of words."

Like a dark thick-leaved tree
I shiver as I fly in bliss,
Unnerved by new-won liberty.
Long days like glow-worms shine
Beneath the creeping vine.

Where the bee sucks, where the spider makes
Its gray silk thread—fine, cobweb-line—
Where the blue hair of ocean shakes
Spells from a noon-struck sky,
There unconfined I lie.

But ever in the Master's vanished eyes
Birds, flowers, beasts, and stumbling Caliban
Live as if summoned to a last assize.
Now no thing artless as before—
The wizard's wand had touched the
    undiscovered shore!

Pietà

FOR THERESA DE KERPELY

Now let the rivers rise and overflow
The banks of love—see how the cold streams rise
From your weeping eyes.
The wound in your calm breast
Carries no telltale stain.
So sacred is your pain,
Let the grave hold it, let the bleeding ground
Receive it, let the weeping sound
Of men and rivers murmur endlessly—
Let the gold seasons breathe it, and the snow
Answer with the lily's glow.

Mary, whose name floats on the bright river
Bright in your Son's grace,
Now that you see His face
Always—beyond the shadow of pain
Yours always and forever—let His smile
Warm you in heaven, now that embracing gaze
Envelops you in love, now all your tears
Drop in the fount of healing, now His breath
Is in the air we breathe; now, now, we know
How courage, courtesy, and charm prevails
When power and brute force fails.
Even in the pits of darkness pray for us,
Pray for us in the darkness and the light.

The Seal of Fire

And he said, I have put this seal
On your breast, on your arm;
You shall never come to harm
She said (and the furies smiled—
Lovely their faces, mild not wild—
The proud and elegant furies cryptic-eyed,
And they never saw these lovers where they lay,
How the wind blew their lives away)

As a seal upon your heart
In fire, in rosy flame
I shall write your name
(She said) and the way to glory lies clear
In this crystal burning year
(He said) in the bright autumnal weather
When the long streams run clear
And the red gold leaves are shed
From the faint blue of the sky,
I shall write our names in fire,
He said, she said,
They said together.

Girl in a Library

The libraries consumed by passionate eyes—

Warm, eager eyes consumed by the dry print—
Years lost in avid reading till the world,
Its landscapes and its figures and its thought,
Stretched to a room's span.

The rushing years
Greet you with scorn who lift your frightened glance
To where the young Spring crescent of the moon
Seeks Venus her companion in the heavens—
Rain-pure and sure, they spill their beauty down
Till the closed suburbs gain a wilder air.

And now the whirling library seems cold,
Drained of its life's blood, now the eyes
Gather delights no more to feed the mind—
Only the young flesh mourns, the sensuous mind
Pines for the storm, dreams of the sun's embrace.

Whose was that restless shadow on the wall?

Song for Three Voices

So fades the glory of this world,
Honor dissolves and pleads no more
But flies beyond the pale.
You shall live to be fourscore.
None shall believe the ancient tale
That you were Thaïs and Jane Shore
And the much sung Iseult.
Who shall believe it when the rain
Of years falls once and then again?
Leveled is the trampled plain—
The hollowed ground is green again.

2ND VOICE:
But never again that face! that face!
A new world rises in its place.

3RD VOICE:
How can we forget that thing
We made true in our memory?
History is another thing.
Now the well-trained voices sing
Their ironic elegy
And the river widening
Guides each legend to its source.
The flying huntsman spurs his horse
Into streams of beauty—where
All who drank were sickened there.
The river races from its course.

Voices in Air

Do you remember? (one said) and they rose from their
     long sleep,
The mock tournament, the feast, and the smile in my eyes
When I pinned the trophy on your breast;
I cannot remember the rest.
Do you remember? (he said) that it was winter then
And the horses were waiting, eager to depart
But the long banquet hall was lit with a thousand lights
And your cloudy silver gown was sprayed
With starlight, moonlight
And we danced the hours away.

Never to meet again we parted:
The trumpets blew the centuries away
And now on clouds of fire, of fiery snow we sing
Of what the hastening seasons sometimes bring.

I remember the hours (she said) when January turned
    to May—
Fancy and wit and ease made holiday
(He said) that glowing winter day,
Then into my saddle I sprung—

We were both destined to die young.

So in the clouds, so on the glimmering Hudson's air
They whispered and rose through naked cloudforms
    changing there,
Reliving one moment out of endless time,
Marking one season always in their rhyme.

The Garden at Cliveden

(Germantown, Pennsylvania, 1777)

January not June. Then why the scent
Of wild heliotrope, of pale yellow roses;
Why ghostly music, and a measured dance
Of graceful shadows under the evening moon?
Then rise those phantoms whose vitality
Is greater than the living, whose quick bloodstream
Is poured from the hectic moon. O thou Selene, Queen
Of the sleeping senses, do not scatter them,
Two lovers who now cross the garden, halt, embrace.

The centuries roll back, and yesterday
Is one with the flooded grass, one with the agile grace,
The quick retentive mind, that almost-caught
Genius from the compelling moon, subtle prophetic
            thought
From captive tides, from sharp air, from moving rivers,
From each distinctive season's special dower;
And one with the shy smile and delicate face,
One who loves more, one who loves less.
The season does not prosper. Selene does not bless
Her lovers, and her cold indifferent charm
Weaves the rough coils of hovering tragedy
With frustrate beauty of the sleeping moon.

Now locked (a moment) in each other's arms
They move and then dissolve in history,
The wars, the eternal wars shall separate;
The dead must strew the garden, gunshot beat
Against the window panes, the bloodstains on the grass
Linger for centuries, lightly as autumn petals

Fall from a withering tree. So shall your loves pass—
One shall remember always—one forget.

And then how beautiful in memory
That winter scene, that arrested glow, when all
Was fulfilled in time, when all that ought to be
Took place in time, fulfillment of all passion
Under the moon, under the hostile moon
Beneath the living heavens, under the unfriendly stars.

Four Ghosts

Four ghosts now walk the Russian forests, girls
Made of fine mists, rain-showers, snow-empearled
Angels of the snowy wastes, wraiths of a dead star,
The murdered daughters of the Czar.

Each with a blood-stained ruby on her breast.
The frozen forest knows them, and the lilac-tinted snow:
The Siberian depths receive them and unblest
In flying death, the imperial eagles freeze—
Trapped in foreordained mortality. The East and West
Tire of their dying cries, but strange unrest
Through historic skies, echo the fatal melodies.

The blood-stained jewels on each breast will burn
Till the last eagle fails and the last shriek;
Till the soul's winter melts, and resurrection blows
Toward that spiked peak where no compassion flows.

The Seven Shadows

FOR JOANNA

The seven shadows hiding in the green wood,
White in glittering sunbreak stood,
Blinking, leaf-pale as white roses are
Star-pale, celestial, neither flesh nor blood,

Who now looked on the sun for the first time,
Golden and fecund, saw how its brilliant look
Pulsed at its center like a beating clock,
Struck sun-dazed shadows on each flying dress,

Gazed on the sun, the sun, so long denied
Diaphanora clad in mist; you, Luminosa; you,
Light-swathed Sylvia, bride of the forest's glimmering
        green;
Rosalba bathing in the freshest dew;

And Cunegunda stepping forth in pride,
Queen of the Gothic solitudes and the trees
That in the chequered forest shades abide
Where bird-crowned trees shake down their leafy
        harmonies;

Atalanta of the white breast and whiter brow
At whose light step the sleeping forest wakes;
Olympia on whose breast faint as the rose-pale snow
Lie curled in amity, two emerald-headed snakes.

Into the cathedral forests where the leaves
Sing and are never still for murmuring
The violet-shaded myrtle droop and spring
In trembling silence where the night bird grieves.

Yet the seven shadows must aspire to light,
Light, light, unshadowed, light unhaunted, calm
For a leaf's breath they fly, from star-struck night
Hesitant between the cypress and the palm.

They leave tree empires to unpeopled air,
Leave the bird worlds to flight, fear, fantasy
To bathe in tropic suns, to comb their blue-black hair
In visionary light, realms without history.

Brooks in Eden

They have never known the precarious, slippery streets
Where your foot falls, nor the long frozen river
You watch chill day by day, till motionless, stark,
The embankment seems to burn with icy fever
Once there were ships that passed, now they are gone.

They will return! O brooks in Eden, cold and pale,
I know the river that you join, where cold and pale
You unite in a silver gleam, mingle in sunstruck streams.
It is always summer in our secret dreams.

I know this scene will brighten, the snow melt
In visions of summer grass and dewdrunk flowers.
Who would have thought in the dead winter season
When the ice refused to melt and the windows shook
That the brooks were waiting in Eden? That it would
    soon be summer?

Hymn to Artemis, the Destroyer

Gray-eyed huntress in whose hair
The crescent moon unquiet lies,
Descending from your mountain stair
Spare the frightened hart—O spare
The warm heart that atrophies.

Under your moon-clouded gaze
The pearl-tipped, star-bright bow we see,
Winging into sterile days,
Days devoid of hope and praise
Never fruitful, wide, or free.

Ah your blazing, stinging, arrow—
Chastity's too rigid flame!
The freezing dove, the starving sparrow
Flying, fall, and call your name.

Now from your cold mountain top
You descend—the harried deer
Spill their lifeblood, drop by drop:
All life's glowing motions stop
In an ecstasy of fear.

But the escaping soul that flies
Into warmer courts of air,
Remembering your moon-shaded eyes
And your heaven-breathing hair,
Ever for your presence sighs.

Imprisoned Chimes

The bells you heard in your youth
Ring when you are away—
From what green chapel or bell-tower
Do they fall on the ear, on the heart,
Tremble from aerial heights, display
What you never wished to say?

Falling music, drum-beat tone
Through an ancient city,
There where the past was overthrown
And the future cheerful and bright, when love
Beckoned you to a dazzling sky,
A blue pavilion and arcade—
There rang the bell-clear ditty
While the chimes off-beat strayed.

Because your heart was light as lace,
Bright-spangled as the dew,
Thoughtless devotion bathed your face
With silver motions, happy grace
The green chapels welcomed you
To their singing place.

And in a virgin wilderness,
Pealing with tumbling waterfalls,
The everlasting rhythm calls
In a divine excess
Loud, clear and bold
Of blazing scarlet, ringing gold.

The Year of the Roses

My roses shrivel in the sun.
I saw them tremble in the sky
Bright with dew, and fresh and young:
Now fall their petals brown and dry,

Flowers of the day! whose beauty sprung
From the cold radiance of the world
When its first noonday race had run—
The tight bud shimmered, then uncurled

Into such perfume, ripeness, grace
It made one hour, one day, one place
An enchanted island in the sea
Of life's contracting mystery.

Perfect the weather, soft the air,
There for a while the long hours run
Naked, rose-scented in the sun:
No shadow of the evening there,

Luminous islands of the blessed;
Fallen these moments cold and clear,
Year of the quivering rose, the year
When what is loved is most possessed.

Two Adaptations from Hölderlin

I

And you Diotima, who walk humbly among the living
Holy, obscure, and pure, a goddess among barbarians
Men know you not—vainly you seek your kindred,
Your sky-born equals.

Sages, and martyrs, virgins who have walked
In supernatural fields of living green,
Paradise's closed arbor where the few,
The sacred few, pluck Paradisal flowers.

But from the dead, the great and tender dead
Who dropped from sensual time and live
In aerial splendor with the darker gods,
Expect your tribute.

They wait to welcome you and my poor song
Lost in a whirlwind clime, you hardly hear.
It sings to drowsy ears, but names you now,
The name you bear in Heaven.

II

Too long we lived for work and wages, we
Have walked among the thorns, ignored the roses
But the day, the day is at hand so long in coming.
The cloud-filled world ignites, is full of light,
The air is alive with birds. All the trees are in flower.
The white flowers kept for the last are grown
Though they seemed to droop—alive on the living tree
We can pluck them now. The rains have restored their
        beauty:
The violets that were crushed, revive again.

And the birds multi-colored, fall from azure clouds
And raise their choral music to the sun—
Darkness has fled while we slept. New skylines arise
Unknown to mortal eyes. It is forever summer.

It will always be light. We have forgotten the night:
Time was, time is, and this one world remains
When the light of evening turns to purple and gold
In the storm, in the pure rain.

O ultimate beauty piercing heart and brain!
Enlighten us, slow-moving moon; and you, O diamond
Bright falling stars, strong ever-moving sea,
Glide on with us, beyond us, toward the light.

Eight Variations on Themes by Petrarch

I

Love, Love, cruel Love, long have you driven me
To follow the wild beast who drives you too
Where the dawn flowers in that exquisite blue
Of cloud and sealine on our summer shore—
The country that we lost and still adore—
From that country of hope, in fertile sunlight laid,
We have brought back dead sea fruit, the sea anemone
And tarnished jewels, broken instruments
That made clear music once and may again—
So beautiful your joy, so rare your pain:
I long for them again and long in vain
And now from shuttered skylights, still I see
How the young, the beautiful, still flock to thee.

I I

With sleep, with all evasion possible,
Naked and poor you go, my hidden spirit
To the deep fountains of old Helicon
Where the bright tree shoots up in limpid water
And where the bird of morning ever springs
On the light heart and spreads its glittering wings.

Deep in a grove of laurel weeping lies
The sacred Muse, Apollo's lyric daughter,
Since Laura's soul descended to the skies—
Who led her dance, who learned her secret tongue
(Alas poor Muse! your summer days are long)
Since Laura sleeps—through empty days she goes
Where the still waves on the encroaching desert flows.

III

There in the gay season, pale and cold,
A young girl stands beneath a laurel tree;
The sun had left her but her face and hair
Shone in the orchard where she used to dance
Under the tree, the sacred laurel tree,
Beneath the branches where gold apples hang.

So peaceful and serene her spirit seemed
That all things turned to flowering sprays of fire,
There, where once bright Apollo tuned his lyre
The notes of beauty, hope, fulfillment rang
Since in that world, the bird of morning sang.

And from green-haunted waves silent ran out
A waiting boat, guarded by Loves; I went
And floated toward some stranger element
Toward the lost continents, the ocean floor
And found myself alone on Memory's shore.

IV

I sing the hand that reached to enclose my fate;
Soft-skinned, snow-soft, soft-gloved so charmingly
That light gloved hand in springtime conquered me:
A hand so small to enfold my destiny!

And I sing the eyes, the brow, the frown, the smile
That held all grace, desire, all innocence,
Lulled by the falling waters of our death
As if the pristine world had caught its breath.

How far, how far away was the season of snow
And I prayed to Time, Time who allots to us
A moment when the senses sting and glow—

A world of opening springs and wavering hope—
And then reveals the scaffold and the sky
An abyss of threatening years, the hangman's rope,
And leaves us stranded on a perilous slope.

V

That was the day I saw the fatal rope
Coiled in a hand of ivory and of snow
Behind a curtain of dark. I hear my tired blood flow
But the white hand still beckons, beckons me.

Sweet is the bait it offers to the soul:
I follow the veiled dark, I bless that hand, and walk
Into a garden where all light has gone
And on invisible waters a lone swan
Praises the hand that dealt the sweetest wound
And then a golden bird sings overhead
In that deep silence where all song has fled
Extolling bells that rise from earth and toll,
Praising the waters for their healing sound—
And still the two birds sing and will not fly
Through that pure darkness to the brooding sky.

V I

In a violet gown, in an azure stole
Star-glittering, carrying a crocus spear,
The Goddess walks the mornings of the year
Following the Phoenix, the Arabian bird.

Following the bird whose flames of golden fire
Must forge the jewel for the Muse's throat,
The Muse I have most invoked, burning with heat,
    with blood,
Whose language I at last have understood.

Before I fail, the Goddess promised me
That I shall walk her grove, wear her attire
Woven of dewclear skies, heaven's softest hue,
And drink the morning, taste infinity—
And see the golden bird of Paradise
Rise once and deathless to my waiting eyes!

VII

As I approach the last of all my days,
How small my world! How large its burden and pain!
And Love, whose charming face I wooed in vain,
Mocks me at last, eludes my yearning gaze.
Angry, embittered now, at your request
I'll sing no more. O Love—your silver chain
I'll now unclasp—go forth now as you came,
A naked child exposed to wind and rain.

And in the dreamless world I'll lie at rest
Since Love must die; then all things too must fall,
All earthly sorrow and resentment flies,
I see at last how worthless was the prize
I sought so long—so slight the sight, the touch—
We die for that which cannot matter much.

VIII

THE DOE AND THE LADY

In a glade of emerald where the shade
Glowed in the moongilt air of evening
A milk-white doe I saw, leaping through air and light
And brilliant as the waterfall her eyes,
Her topaz-tinted eyes.

Pale woman facing all your vanished beauty,
Where has it gone? why did this flying doe

Shed such a running trail of harmony,
A world of opening skies and glittering dew
On the sky-silvered blue?

In diamond letters on a collar of gold
Across the doe's white neck I saw inscribed,
"Touch me at your peril, hinder not,
For my great sovereign the last king of kings,
The sky-descended, earth-engrossing emperor,
The Caesar of this world, the scourge of worlds to
    come,
Has left me free to roam the imagined world."

And now this doe roams through the flying air
And views through northmost outposts of despair
The green-gloomed, rock-rimmed sea.
And follows storms that fiercely urge her on
Into the rough-hewn ocean, where her gaze
Pierces the treacherous rockpools, where sea-flowers
Cast off their frozen powers.
Or where cool, cool, in chastity and dark
A seagirl's form is seen swift, flying, white
In deep insistent light
Casting white spells of healing and delight.

Then like a wind storm, fainter, lighter growing,
Swooning and drowning with the storm-bolt hour,
Her white breast like the moon, and ocean rises
To seaflow and to light.

Capture the doe, and draw it by surmise
To face the tempest dying in our eyes—
There in our captive eyes where all drowned beauty
    flows,

The Heavenly Beast that never knows repose
Through emerald thickets flying,
Or where the Snow King's daughters
Rise on the angry waters.

Cardinal Pietro Bembo (14 7 0 –15 4 7)

(On the death of his brother)

You, too, my brother in your hour of Spring
Left me too suddenly as if compelled
Lightly, and with a golden glittering—
As if your sparkling life was caught and held
In the large hand of time and dropped untimely where
Your eager world dissolves in the high air.
All that was wild and gay is now nowhere
And I, reflected in your eyes, shone too.
My mirrored shadow living in your grace,
Lived for a moment in your living face,
Now into silence, into death's disgrace,
Final injustice that gives none his due:
I too would leave my place, and follow you.

From the Italian of Gaspara Stampa (1523–1554)
(Mesta e penitia dei miei gravi errori)

With deep repentance for my wasted days,
Trivial thoughts and sensual desires
Squandering away my days, these few rare days
Of fugitive life to kindle dying fires.
To You, to You, my God in my despair
I turn at last and let Your flaming snow
Upon my heart in sacred ardor glow—
Stretch forth Your hand, for I am shipwrecked, float
In a black whirlpool, drifting, sinking, gone:
A ghost that rains and tempests beat upon,
I mourn my sins, I beg Your aid once more,
Hopeful I turn, O weeping I deplore;
You who for all mankind did suffer loss
Desert me not, lean down from Your high cross.

From the Italian of
Michelangelo Buonarroti (1475–1564)

My soul without a friend, without a guide,
Teaches me slowly, slowly, O too slow
To feel another's sorrow, and my pride,
Dear Lord of Fate! has made me shun Thy flag
Beneath whose sign, Your wounded legions go.

No triumph, Lord of Fate, but it is Thine—
Then lift my spirit, Lord, its slow decline
Has made my blood run low, my strivings lag
And tamed my talents grown too thin and fine.

Coward I am, who fears to see the light,
I hide within my art, while Time takes flight,
Too harsh to others, are my sins so light?

Mercy! I cry, O see my wound, my scar,
Too close I am to death, from God too far.

From the Italian of
Lorenzo de' Medici (1 4 4 8 –1 4 9 2)
(*Vida madonna sopra in fresco rio*)

Beside a running brook my lady stands,
Green branches arched above her, and the skies
Reflected in the silver running tide.
Her face is seen as in an illumined book
Shadowed by evening winds when night demands
That all things end, when only night abides.
Forever stands her image now, it holds
That primal passionate look.

I saw in her young face, in her proud air
All time, all seasons run, the earth had veiled
All things, my youth, my sorrow, and my flame,
My love, my longing, and my honored name.

Now always when the early spring revives
Memory, memory, lasting memory—
I feel this morning sweetness, pause and sway
Into a world of fountains, dancing spray
Where the inspiring vision still endures,
Nor like the stream shall ever float away.

A Theme from Louise Labé

Diana sleeping under the flowering apple tree
I saw in the green orchard. She arose
In wrath at my approach and said to me,
"Nymph, nymph, where are your weapons for the chase,
These silver arrows my sworn maidens bear?
Now leave this singing green, this fertile valley.
Tomorrow all my girls go to the race.
The wild boars rage on the mountains, in the hollow
The panthers prowl, the sleek deer follow."

My weapons are all gone, O virgin queen,
My quiver broken, and my sandaled feet
Limp wounded. In a covert deep and green
A stranger seized my quiver and my arrows.
Beautiful he was and bold, and his touch harsh and hot;
He took my bow and aimed shot after shot
On my open heart. His indifferent laughter rings
Long after he has left. And the wound stings.

A Song with Refrain

The mid-century rocks: its figures rise,
Madman, hesitant saints, whose eyes
Close on the brutal world and silently
Perform with grace their miracle and depart
But leave a blessing on the astonished heart:
Time, time, alone can thwart and threaten me.

All lives find their one miracle, to all will come
The angel with the lifted branch who cries
(Where one will hear), "Arise and follow me,
Among the whirlpools of obscenity
The evils that you feared face you, and fly:
Pandora's box is broken, imprisoned demons rise,
Unseen but half-revealed life's delicate mystery."
Time, time, alone, sustains and strengthens me.

Soon all the candles burn, soon all our loves are known,
Foeman and friend are one—
Beyond the precinct of the obscuring sun,
Among the olive trees and lilies He
Reveals the oasis in the furthest sea.
When all is done, done well, and secretly—
Time, time alone, has tamed and ravished me.

In the old cities, in the furthest sea,
In the wild conflict, in the frustrate sigh,
In troubled visions of futurity,
When mind and soul are dry
I bless the visible world's security,
Even You, even You, my ancient enemy.
Time, time, alone has charmed and conquered me.

Each season finds its miracle; I know
Where the seed flies, where the wind blows

The price is reckoned (ah the price of blood!)—
It is of God and cannot be withstood.
The earth grows like a tree, the heart is free;
It too, grows old, grows gray, like the old sea
It pays its tribute to mortality.
Time, time, alone reveals, enlightens me.

The Snowy Woods

The woods are lapped in snow,
The leveled buried plain;
They once were mine I know.
Familiar slept the grain
Planted so long ago.

Through hostile oceans now
I passed and once again
In my mild evening glow
Once more I see the rain
Flowing from ice and snow.

Land of my childhood where
I never flowered or grew.
The slow ebb in my blood
Quickens to answer you.

Skies where my first thoughts knew
Life's magic view
And the first lyric rains
Against cold window panes--

I mount your aerial stair
Reaching into nowhere

The white snow on my hair.

Song

Life with her weary eyes,
Smiles, and lifts high her horn
Of plenty and surprise;
Not so where I was born

In the dark streets of fear,
In the damp houses where greed
Grew sharper every year
Through hunger and through need.

Lest the harsh atmosphere
Corrode, defeat, destroy
I built a world too clear,
Too luminous for joy.

Unnatural day on night
I built—tall tower on tower,
Bright on supernal light
Transfixed the too-bright flower.

But see how it has grown!
The cold dream melts, the frost
Dissolves—the dream has sown
A harvest never lost.

Blood runs into the veins,
The wild hair in the wind
Waves in the natural rains;
The harsh world and unkind

Smiles, and its eye grown mild
Surveys this nothingness
Like an indifferent child
Too sleepy to undress.

New Poems

Chorale for the Seasons

In the time of the scorpion we first came
To the forests floating in light, and the swaying shadows
Sun-dipped in moving gold,
Leaving despair behind, and a dark season,
The sting of malice, and the dangerous door,
O my bright scorpion!

Beautiful it was in the year of the Ram,
The wild flowers opening in love to the sun, the trees wavered
Warm in trembling air, fanning the seablue heaven:
There the children were always in white, and always singing
Oh my beautiful ones!
Time drew her curtain down, and veiled the scene.

It was best to live in the time of the running deer
Soft-eyed and wary, peering behind dark thickets
Or leaping through mist-wrapped mountains drinking in cool
        hollows,
O my doe with the fearful eyes!
It was your year of illusion, white is your shade on the moun-
        tain.

Slowly we wheeled into the cycle of the wild swans
When the rain flooded the earth, and the children departing
Spread their soft wings to the light, ascended to thundering
        heavens;
Left alone to the quiet of the moon, to the whirling waters,
Beautiful swans we salute you—
Flying into the unknown, landing in virgin skyscapes,
Exploring unborn stars.

Drifting, sauntering, see we have reached
The world of the water lilies

Only in dreams, when the spirit released, leaves her un-
    wanted body
When the sun is obscured, and the night prepares
To unveil her starry shores—
In the white trance of the moon
O my white and golden lilies!

Now is the time when the demon that hides in the clouds,
The seawraiths that wail in the waters,
The storm spirits chained in the shaking woods,
Mix with the scorpions, mate with the wild swans,
Call to the golden Ram who grows fat in a prosperous
    meadow;
Timid the white doe drinks, returns to the shimmering pool
Where the young stars are drowning.
Drift like the stars, my soul,
My white and drifting lily.

Homage to Christina Rossetti

Silence of after-wars, when through the air
The high, leaf-dropping tree
Reflects the bright blue weather glowing there,
So still, so quiet your fame, diffusèd, yet nowhere:

Your dark Italian streams of English song
Poured such clear fountains down,
Delicate as a string of fine-matched pearls, as strong
As the fretted iron in the great Tuscan's crown:

And fresh as young-eyed seasons of the mind
When the heart bathes in sun and clouded streams grow
    clearer,
Or when the grave and golden autumns find
God's contemplative beauty closer, nearer.

Then best we praise you for your garlands' shading,
Death's feet and Love's, garlands of small, perfect roses,
Small roses few but perfect, never fading,
Brought from your secret heavens, startling our garden
    closes.

For you the Sacred Muse revealed her illumined way
And taught the single heart, devout and true,
How to praise God in fire-touched songs that pray,
Songs that Teresa heard, Siena's Catherine knew.

Then like a garland of pearls, or a stream of gold,
Or a great pillar of fire, or a small, wounded bird,
Your quiet gifts rang purest gold,
Rang finest silver, and were loved, were heard.

Spellbound

I looked and saw your life
In the shadow of your hair,
In the glory of your eyes—
Bells, bells, rang everywhere
On the storm-threatened air.

I looked and saw a light
In the shadow of your brow,
In the white power of your hand,
A whirl of wind and snow
Where golden angels stand
Gleaming against the night.

This was the moment when trees
Lifted their April arms
In a pale rush of green
Shading a moonlit scene
Casting their early charms
And their newborn dreams
In magic streams.

O then it was I saw
In the shadow of your hair,
In the dark power of your eyes,
The magnetic pull of the sea—
Earth's spellbound mystery
Strict in its changing law.

The World of the Salamanders

Slowly, and one by one, with few to see or hear
Above the chilling movement of the sea
The salamanders dripping gold appear.

Through trembling waters, over primal seas
They arise, and sing of fire, of fire-lit phantasies;
They summon marvels, legends, mysteries.

Then arise at their command from wind and wave
Divas, Peris, water-pale Undines
And mist-veiled weeping queens.

In wavering worlds of sleep, in the skull's cave
    they sing
A *gloria* in honor of their king.

Metaphysics of the Night

Our bones are scattered at the grave's mouth,
Our lives have fled before the certain tread
Of Time, she of the multiple disguises, she
Who in her many forms is never still.

How fresh and gay among the daffodils
In the April season by a gleaming river
We saw her first, quick, ardent, saffron-robed,
Free as the air, a dryad with sunstruck hair
Who moved in a green world, plucking white flow-
    ers.

White rose on fire! moss rose in a damp meadow
She seemed—firebright in a burning season
Green world on fire! air's freedom lightly shadowed
Immortality in modern dress appears
Disguised as Time, was Time, is Time itself
A gay green masquer in a crumbling world.

And now invisible among the stars
I hear her in the murmurs of the tide
Gliding through rainsoaked branches in the park
Hovering over banquets and the dance.

And violet-shadowed in the receding sea
And darkening mild Sunday afternoons
Her spectral image rises and restores
Solitude, certitude, and history.